WANT TO BE A SUPERINTENDENT?

The A to Z Guide to Get You There

HARRY & ELIZABETH REYNOLDS

WANT TO BE A SUPERINTENDENT?
The A to Z Guide to Get You There

Dr. Harry Reynolds & Dr. Elizabeth Reynolds
libysupt@aol.com

ISBN: 978-1-943342-51-8

Printed in the United States of America.
First Edition

Design and Published by: Destined To Publish
www.DestinedToPublish.com

TABLE OF CONTENTS

DEDICATION

This book is dedicated to my parents, Samuel Hill and Effie Dogan Hill, both of whom are deceased, and to my brothers and sisters, most of whom began their careers teaching: Jackie, Celestine, Shirley (Dr. Hilliard), Patricia, Thomas (Brother), Rebecca, Virginia, and Samuel (Jr.).

It is with much love and appreciation that I say thank you to my daughter Erna, my son Samuel, my granddaughter Aaliyah, my assistant John Perez, and other colleagues and associates.

The encouragement of family has been priceless. I thank them for their prayers and support of this book and other publications. Additionally, thank you to my sister Dr. Shirley Hill Hilliard, and colleague Dr. Carole Collins Ayanlaja for the time they contributed proofing this manuscript. Also, thanks to the many teachers, principals, administrators, superintendents, and boards who worked with us over our years of service to children.

Dr. Elizabeth H. Reynolds

•

To my late mother, Dorothy L. Solomon, whose formal education was limited. I would like to thank her for the sacrifices she made in order that I might receive the education that she was denied. She took enormous pride in the achievements of her son (Harry). Though her formal education ended in eighth grade, she was an avid reader and a learner. Peace, Love, and Admiration.

Dr. Harry J. Reynolds

We started writing this book before the novel coronavirus pandemic in 2020. Students said goodbye abruptly. Once-in-a-lifetime events, like senior proms, were called off. Traditional graduation rituals gave way to socially distanced or virtual celebrations of the end of high school. We were involved because our granddaughter was scheduled to graduate high school. The heartbreak that comes from graduating during the pandemic was rough, but the Class of 2020 was resilient, and so were their educators, finding new ways to make the moment meaningful and memorable *(Education Week, June 2020)*. Our granddaughter was involved in a drive-through high school graduation. We returned home to take pictures with our family, only in our driveway and on our lawn. Many graduations involved drive-ins, park-ins, and car parades. The world seemed to stop as things seemed to be spinning out of control.

As educators and leaders, we almost always want control of our schedules and events; however, this COVID-19 pandemic was something we could not control. This was the first time in the history of education that a virus was calling the shots, and we could not do one thing about it. The COVID-19 pandemic has school leaders searching for ways to continue to educate their students, keep their schools and districts safe, and "keep the fiscal ship afloat amid plummeting revenues, unexpected costs, and state and local budget uncertainty" *(Education Week, June 2020)*. This was a perfect time to understand that there are some things in life that we can control and some that we have no control over. One advantage of dealing with this crisis is that it has forced us to become experts at virtual learning, virtual coaching, virtual professional development, virtual keynotes, and virtual web conferences.

FOREWORD

This book was written to share with you the A through Z real-life experiences we encountered while serving as Superintendents. It is important that you understand what motivated us to take on the role of Superintendent and why we decided to continue to serve in the position year after year after year.

This book is not a 10 or 12-step chronicle for you to follow and then, zoom, you are ready. Not the case. Rather, this document is shared in an A to Z order, through our eyes as teachers. This publication reflects a myriad of our experiences mixed with the wisdom that we have gained through serving successfully as Superintendents over the years. Thanks for allowing us to share an abundance of good information with you in order to help you understand what the life of a Superintendent entails.

If you are reading this book, then you are curious about what we have written, or perhaps you are interested in becoming a Superintendent if your heart is set on serving in that role. We hope that you have given considerable thought to what this goal might mean in terms of your future preparation. Our purpose is to assist you in understanding the importance of acquiring a strong knowledge base, as well as gaining the skills needed for winning and serving in the position successfully year after year. In addition, it is essential that we bring to your attention the problems, issues, and trivial mishaps that can easily pull you away from your position of Superintendent.

As Christians, we use our moral and ethical compass to guide our decision making, and much of our philosophy and sentiments are influenced by scripture. Furthermore, we have always tried to do what was in the best interest of the children we have served, not necessarily what was politically correct, which can sometimes become extremely difficult. At the beginning of each chapter is a scripture, and many are referenced throughout the book. Consider these ancient spiritual writings to be tools in your leadership toolbox that may be used as a part of your frame of reference. They have worked well for us.

Being an engaged leader can be a challenge for some Superintendents because they may not be accustomed to "getting their hands dirty" with the front-line heavy lifting that is required to change the course of a district. Neither of us feared working in the trenches. Our pathways have survived many unexpected bumps and turns. But we have kept our focus on our purpose: to serve communities with our hearts and our minds.

As you delve into reading this book, you may sense that (maybe like yourself, or perhaps not) we started from ordinary working-class families. The greatest gift our families could give us was a commitment to hard work and ethical character, and they did both. Education was a cornerstone in our families, and we were inspired to teach as young people. Through our commitment to the classroom, we developed a deep partnership with schools. This alliance with education and an embedded dedication to improving it prompted us to parlay our classroom talent into other educational leadership roles. We sought progressively more challenging and complex positions throughout the years because we believed and still do believe in the value of excellence in education. From the beginning of our teaching careers, many of our superiors recognized our talent and leadership potential. When offered opportunities to lead, we did not shy away from the challenges. No strangers to fear and not afraid to be fearless, we accepted each new option. As the saying goes, we were always given opportunities that we could not refuse.

While we came from different backgrounds and family structures, we both have a common ethic that binds us. Personally and professionally, we are genuinely passionate about what we do, and both of us have high expectations for ourselves and for those we have led. Our formative years gave us our unique stories that have been impactful to our past and present and will continue to shape our future. In this book, we share our heartfelt reflections with you to give you encouragement in your leadership walk. We have been molded by what each of us experienced and contributed as teachers, administrators, and superintendents.

Thank you for joining us on this journey, one that allows us to walk with you as professional partners and supporters, sharing seeds of knowledge that we have gained. We proudly walk behind you also, with the hopes that what we share will help push you forward and propel you to great success and satisfaction as a Superintendent.

Harry & Elizabeth

"Success is not measured by what you accomplish, but by the opposition you have encountered, and the courage with which you have maintained the struggle against overwhelming odds."

- Orison Swett Marden -

WHO IS A
SUPERINTENDENT?

A school district Superintendent is the Chief Executive Officer of the district and is responsible for its overall performance. Essentially, serving as the CEO, they are the face of the district, the person most responsible for its success, and most assuredly liable when there is failure. The role is broad; it can be rewarding, but it can sometimes become a nightmare if the Superintendent's capacity to perform is limited or the climate needed to support their actions is nonexistent. The decisions a Superintendent makes can be difficult and taxing. Thus, it takes an exceptional person expertly prepared to use their unique skills and be effective in the role (Derrick Meador, "Examining the Role of an Effective School Superintendent," *ThoughtCo*, June 30, 2019).

The day-to-day responsibilities of the Superintendent are expansive. Hiring new teachers, ensuring that current teachers have up-to-date certifications, following continuing education requirements, and ensuring that the students excel put a lot of responsibility on the individual holding this position. Larger school districts or smaller ones with adequate resources often have both a Superintendent and an Assistant Superintendent in tandem as a team. The main job of the Superintendent is to coordinate the various educational goals set by the state and the school board. The Superintendent's position is typically filled through either a community election or an appointment by the school board. (Usually, as a part of a national search, this search firm is hired specifically to provide candidates for the board to interview.) In addition to overseeing the staff of the school system, superintendents are also responsible for budgeting, curriculum design, human resources, and facility management.

The assistant superintendent may be focused on curriculum and instruction, facilities management, special services, or human resources education.

Superintendents "must ensure that the students under their supervision have top-notch education and a safe environment, from physical safety to nutrition to enacting anti-bullying measures. Superintendents are also required to work within parameters that may include state and federal curricula requirements and available budgets. Effective communication skills and a strong ability to prioritize are essential for success in this position" ("School District Superintendent: Education, Salary, and Outlook," *Resilient Educator*).

WHAT DO SUPERINTENDENTS REALLY DO?

Superintendents are managers and leaders in charge of directing themselves and others toward what the district needs to serve students best. But the tasks of a Superintendent are not as important as their temperament. As the face of the district, Superintendents set the tone for the district. No doubt, one of their most important roles involves communication with constituents. Superintendents are "responsible for hiring and supervising the other administrators in the district, including the chief financial officer and the school principals," to name a few. The superintendent must also respond to the demands of all stakeholders in the district: the teachers, students, parents, staff, and the community at large. Money is always at the forefront, how the dollars are acquired and spent. Superintendents "must consider how to allocate the financial and human resources of the district in order to achieve the best results. While being mindful of all the competing demands, a great superintendent will ultimately be guided by a singular question: What is best for all students?" ("What Makes a Great Superintendent?" *GreatSchools*, September 14, 2010).

SO, ARE
YOU QUALIFIED?

The qualifications for a Superintendent range from experience with financial analysis to strong interpersonal skills and professional communication. Superintendents have to juggle many different responsibilities, and because of this, a disciplined approach to priorities and time management is key. Charisma and the ability to rally broad-based support is critically important.

Effective Superintendents are focused on the students—the main topic on their agenda. The effective Superintendent serves students well and delivers on a promise of providing an outstanding education for all students. This is what a community expects and will support, nothing less. The research on leadership has provided Superintendents with a relatively clear understanding of the fundamental principles of effective leadership. Great schools come about when Superintendents work closely and productively together with all stakeholders in the school district community.

Being an effective Superintendent is dependent upon forming a successful working relationship with an elected group of citizens in a community: the Board of Education. The survival of a Superintendent depends upon the consistent support of the majority of the Board of Education. With that support, the Superintendent can move the district's agenda forward in a rather swift and smooth fashion.

Great schools are created when all individuals involved in education work together in a wise and organized way. There is no perfect community, no perfect school district, no perfect Board of Education, and no perfect Superintendent. Superintendents set themselves up for failure when they think that they won't make mistakes or that they will not need assistance from a cadre of colleagues. They do, and they will.

> **Elizabeth:** The advantage that I had coming into the position of Superintendent was that my husband had served in the position successfully for several years before I started this journey. I had the advantage of bouncing things off of him in every area that I could think of: Board of Education relationships, teaching and learning, strategic planning, parent and community involvement, school finances and balancing a budget, public relations, and dealing with the media, to name a few.

It would be a Superintendent's dream to be consistently supported by the whole Board of Education. Too often, members of Boards of Education assume that their elected position gives them the charge of engaging in decision making regarding all aspects of district leadership. The primary responsibility of board members functioning as a governance body is to vote on policy decisions, approve the budget, and hire the district Superintendent. It is the responsibility of the Superintendent to lead the mission and vision of the district by managing the administrative responsibilities and employees. When the role of the Board of Education and the role of the Superintendent become muddled, this creates obstacles for educational progress—relationships become strained, and lines of communication become blurred.

> **Harry:** I had a dream Board of Education when I first took my job as Superintendent in the state of California. My board allowed me to lead the district smoothly without interruption for six years. This is extremely rare and was such a blessing to me. I was able to accomplish great things.

The Superintendent's job can be one of the loneliest jobs ever, yet also one of the most challenging and fulfilling. It is important that a Superintendent remains humble because, if not, an individual can start "believing his/her own press." That's a problem! When a Superintendent becomes recognized as the visible leader that they are, many people in the district and community will put them on a pedestal. The Superintendent becomes known as "the person," "the expert," the important person in the community. People look up to the leader: parents, students, teachers, principals, administrators, community leaders, clergy, and elected politicians. But, if the tide turns and schools are unsuccessful, or an issue occurs that brings concern to the community, all constituents again look at the leader.

As Superintendent, being approachable is important. People will recognize the Superintendent from media outlets, social media, formal and informal events, and in the neighborhood. Superintendents must remember to remain friendly and down-to-earth, especially to the parents, students, teachers, and all employees. They must be humble and watchful, aware that they are only as strong as their weakest link.

In this book, you will find scenarios from both of us that deal with issues big and small, none less significant than the other. The responsibility of creating ongoing educational success for other people's children in a community requires a focus on that which may appear minute and that which is monumental.

Superintendents share their vision/mission for the district and manage million-dollar budgets. They also bend down and tie the shoelaces of kindergarteners. Most importantly, they set a climate for success.

> **Elizabeth:** It was my expectation that every student move forward in school, having mastered the grade-level content, in order to graduate with all the skills and knowledge necessary to enter post-secondary education or the world of work successfully.

Being a Superintendent is not a job for the faint-hearted or the uncommitted. There will be many days when the feeling of uncertainty about taking the job will be at an all-time high. Those days will likely occur as the aftermath of a necessary decision made by the Superintendent that didn't placate a particular segment of the staff or community. Leadership requires bold moves that are in the best interest of children and families, which means they don't waver based on the demands of a few.

Psalm 30:5 reminds us that "Weeping may endure for a night, but joy cometh in the morning." This is so true because no matter how difficult the Superintendent's day may be, at home at night, relaxation and reflection await. In a state of peace, it is easy to identify why this is a position that calls a strong leader forward. A climate of calm is where leaders gather their thoughts and reassure themselves that tomorrow is another day and the drawing board welcomes a return visit.

> **Elizabeth:** I am reminded that this commitment is all about my students. It is not about me, the Board of Education, or staff. I start to think, "If the students were not here, we wouldn't be here. This business is about kids."

Together, we have shared many stories over our careers. When we started out as teachers, we "had arrived." We did not have any expectation of being anything except excellent teachers. However, as beginning teachers, we were both fortunate to work in districts where we were encouraged, "pushed," and given opportunities to learn and to grow as professionals. We did not know it at the time, but all of our experiences along the way prepared us for the job of Superintendent.

The encouragement we received included appointing us to serve on school site committees, as well as district-wide committees such as textbook committees, curriculum committees, budget committees, social committees, extracurricular activities committees, and various other policy-related committees. In each case, whenever positions were opened and advertised, somehow or another, we were made aware and usually selected. This allowed us to apply ourselves and grow, become more confident, acquire experience with interviewing, and have exposure both with new colleagues and with other leaders/educators and policymakers.

> **Elizabeth:** Harry has served as Superintendent in California, Tennessee (as the first Black Superintendent in Chattanooga), and Illinois, and I have served as Superintendent in Illinois, in three school districts. Together, we have just about half a century of experience in this role: Harry has 25+ years, and I have 20+ years. For some of these years, both of us served as Superintendent at the same time. It is extremely rare for a husband and wife to serve as Superintendents simultaneously; however, it did allow us to compare and contrast our positions and to lean on one another for support. Shop talk has been and continues to be at the dinner table.

Your Superintendent path might be easier than ours, or it might very well be tougher. Doors may close when you thought the job was in the palm of your hand. Remember that wherever you are in your leadership walk, you are blessed to be exactly where you are in your career.

> **Elizabeth:** I was interviewed by a college professor completing a research project on "Superintendents Who Have Staying Power." I was selected; apparently, she realized that I had served as Superintendent for over 15 years. It was an honor for me because I never realized that this individual had served as Superintendent for only one year.

Both of us were taught as children to value our job and to uphold the expectations of the person who made the opportunity possible. Professional courtesy dictates that. This training influenced our attitudes toward the Boards of Education that hired us. We realized early in our careers that we could not let down or disappoint the governing body that gave us a vote of confidence to lead. This is one reason we believe that we have had staying power in a public school district leadership that rotates Superintendents in and out like a revolving door. Some other reasons that we believe contributed to our longevity in the seat are:

- We are blessed to have established a good track record of working well with Boards of Education who knew and understood their role and respected our work.

- We came into the job with strong academic and pedagogical backgrounds.

- Upon being hired as a new Superintendent in all of our districts, we have worked with our Boards of Education to develop a strong working relationship, developing beliefs and expectations for both the Board of Education and the Superintendent. *This usually occurs in a Board of Education/Superintendent retreat or special meeting within the first month we are hired. In some cases, an unbiased consultant was hired to oversee the process.*

- We have subsequently worked with our Boards of Education to develop and approve a strategic plan. *This has usually also been done with an outside consultant. It is always better to select a neutral person. Furthermore, upon arriving as a new Superintendent, we have worked with our Boards of Education to develop and approve a long- and short-range plan, including Board of Education/Superintendent goals and indicators.*

- We have worked with our Boards of Education as they have developed and approved strong board policies and procedures.

- We have kept our channel of communication open to all Board of Education members on a regular basis. *"What one knows, all know." This is critical and will be dealt with in the contents of this book.*

- We have also communicated with individual board members

as needed and with the entire board on a weekly basis. Our manners are professional yet caring.

- We exhibit warm personalities and recognize the importance of communicating well with different types of people, including staff members, so that they know their input matters. We use our charisma. *Kindliness and firmness go hand in hand because people respond to both. "Kindness is a language that the blind can see, and the deaf can hear."*

- We surround ourselves with staff that genuinely shares our vision. *This idea seems obvious. However, you must be able to trust that your team sees exactly what you see at all times. You are only as strong as your weakest link.*

Finally, in this book, we want to share with you the environment that formed our character and personalities and allowed us to become Superintendents of school districts. Neither one of us was born into a society that welcomed us. Segregation in the South did not birth hope. But it created a strong sense of resilience and purpose that guided our actions.

> **Elizabeth:** The environment where Harry was raised was not one in which a young black child would be deciding what he was going to be when he grows up. This was because of the segregation in the workplace during that period. If you know the history of race relations in the United States or have relatives in this country, you will know why.

> **Harry:** Elizabeth grew up in a "traditional" home: mother and father, and eight siblings. She played school with her brothers and sisters because she had a large family to work with. I have always had high expectations for myself. Even though I did not have much when I was growing up, I knew that I wanted to be something "Big," but I didn't know what!

If you believe you have the credentials and requirements listed in the advertisement for the job, do you believe you have the potential to do the job? Are you ready for it mentally and physically? If the answer is yes to each of these questions, then it is time to put yourself out there!

In chapters A-Z, we are going to share information, memoirs, our experiences, and stories from some of our Superintendent colleagues who have survived some of the challenging situations that all Superintendents will face from time to time. Some of the most difficult times you face will make you the best leader in the bunch.

As you read chapters A-Z, there will be tips and ideas about what it takes to become a good Superintendent. In addition to hearing about our experiences as Superintendents, you will hear exciting stories that will motivate and encourage you to go for the position, stay in the position, and stay strong. You are ready to go now. But remember, this is not a sprint. It is a marathon requiring commitment and a huge amount of stamina. Enjoy the ride. For us, the experience as Superintendent has been one of the most thrilling opportunities one can have. It has been a blessing to both of us.

Throughout this book, as you read the scriptures and words of wisdom that have heavily influenced our personal and professional lives, think about the impact they may have on your thoughts and behaviors. It is our hope that you find some tidbits that inspire and invigorate you on your walk to becoming your best Superintendent you! So, let's get started!

MY FORMATIVE YEARS
DR. HARRY J. REYNOLDS

I was born into a dysfunctional poor family, to a 15-year-old unmarried mother. My mother was one of 12 surviving children in a family in which her alcoholic father and his Christian wife reared their children in poverty and eked out a living. Despite our deep poverty, strong ethical and moral values were taught and enforced by our home, church, and school. I was raised in Mixon Town, a poor black neighborhood located on the southwest side of Jacksonville, Florida. Mixon Town was a small community with a mixture of "shotgun" houses, which were owned by landlords, most of whom were middle-class white people who lived in a different neighborhood.

Mixon Town had one schoolhouse for colored children. The school, an ancient wooden two-story "fire trap," covered grades 1-8. Though our neighborhood was economically deprived, it was a pleasant and safe place to be, especially for children and elderly people. Most of our neighbors were long-time residents and were well known and respected in the community. There was a strong respect for the senior members by those who were younger. The mantra in our household was "respect all people without regard for race, age or gender."

Though our community was impoverished, as were the children in our family, we were taught strong values that would carry us throughout our lives. Honesty and fair play were also stressed in our house. My mother's strong desire for learning continued to build into her adult life. She continued her avid desire to read widely and learn from the middle-class and well-educated white families for whom she worked.

I continued performing well in school, and my mother decided to place me in an all-male boarding school in Nashville, Tennessee. I was not happy! After much thought, I realized she was trying to give me a strong education, and additionally, as I later learned, she was making huge financial sacrifices on my behalf. I settled down and went to work, graduating second in my class, which was a great accomplishment.

My mother's wisdom proved to be significantly greater than mine. Placing me in a boarding school population provided opportunities that would not have been available in my local public school.

Had I not attended school in Nashville, I would not have had the strong emphasis on post-high school opportunities or the options that were open to me. I would have missed the strong encouragement from a school population that motivated me to "hang in there."

In late summer, I enrolled as a freshman at City College of San Francisco. For the first time in my life, I attended school with every possible kind of American. I struggled through my first year, learning how to successfully "go to college." I soon learned there were many other struggling young people. I also learned the value of collaborating with other students to gain strength in areas of weakness. Like so many young black students experiencing their first post-high school experience, I lacked the advantage of advice as to which academic courses would open access to different professions. I was advised to study sociology or psychology. I transferred to San Francisco State University as a junior and graduated in two years with a Bachelor of Science degree in Social Science. One year following my graduation from college, I was drafted into the United States Army, trained as a medical corpsman, and assigned to an artillery unit in Germany. While serving my time in the Army, I was sent to a medical academy for advanced training. Upon graduating from the medical academy, I was asked to join the academy staff as a teacher, where I served the remainder of my two-year requirement.

It was during my time in Germany teaching soldiers that I realized I had a real gift and a love for teaching. Though I held the rank of corporal, I was called upon to present to officers and enlisted men. I was able to command and hold their attention during my presentations. Prior to my teaching time in the Army, I had never given any serious thought to education as a profession.

Upon release from the Army after two years, I applied for a variety of jobs and was told, "you are too qualified," "job is filled," etc. I ended up detailing automobiles to earn money. I resolved to prepare for teaching because there was a shortage of teachers at that time, I knew I was good at teaching, and I could gain certification in two years.

After completing the required coursework, I was one of eight graduates assigned to a high school to replace teachers who were scheduled to go on leave the second semester. Late in the second semester, all of us were offered contracts for the next school year. I was excited about my assignment and sought counsel and advice from teachers who had strong reputations. I discovered that some of my colleagues were not anxious to share and relied heavily on worksheets and other devices that showed a lack of creativity. On the other hand, the person on the faculty I found most helpful was the vice principal of instruction. She would walk me through lessons I thought had failed, encouraging me to rethink the lesson and try again. This was so helpful, and it made me more motivated. I was delighted. I learned early on to never get advice from any teacher who was just "floating" through the assignment.

Over a period of six to seven years, I was promoted to junior high counselor, Central Office Project Director, and traveling counselor, working with the "challenged" students of five junior high schools. Most of my caseload involved working with students in an attempt to help them understand how to deal with their peers and teachers in conflict situations.

I was told I would be moved to the new 9-12 in Richmond, California, John F. Kennedy High School, which would be completed and opening the following fall. During this period, I had continued graduate work for a doctorate with a major in curriculum and instruction. The new Superintendent called me in to discuss a new assignment. I shared with him my interest in instruction and was informed that the designated principal wanted someone with whom he had previously served to be the curriculum and instruction person. I was, nonetheless, still selected to become an assistant principal of the school and would be the second in command when the principal was not available.

I made it my business to be very visible on the campus whenever students were out of class. I wanted to know all our students on campus, as well as students not enrolled who wanted to hang around the campus. Over time, my relationship with the student body became extremely powerful. Two years after the opening of the new John F. Kennedy High School, the principal was promoted to Deputy Superintendent when the Superintendent left the district. Finally, I was promoted and became the principal of J.F.K. High School. I served in that role for six wonderful years.

The school district of Oakland is a large multiracial school district on the eastern side of the San Francisco Bay. Nearing the end of my tenure as the high school principal, I received a phone call from the personnel director, who, after some small talk, told me the new Superintendent wanted to see me about a position. Dr. Mark Foster was highly charismatic as a new Superintendent and the first black person to hold the job in Oakland. I was interviewed by Dr. Foster and his administrative cabinet, and they informed me of his intent to reorganize the administrative structure of the district into three regions supervised by three regional Superintendents. After the conversation, I was offered the position of Regional Superintendent of the most challenging, Region #2. This region was the most demanding because it had most of the new government programs instituted by President Lyndon B. Johnson.

In the third year of my tenure as Regional Superintendent, I continued my graduate work at the University of California, Berkeley. I had been excused by the District Office Deputy Superintendent to attend a seminar at the University that conflicted with our regular school board meeting. That evening after my seminar, I returned home and was informed that Dr. Foster, the Superintendent, had been assassinated, and Dr. Bob Blackburn, the Deputy Superintendent, was hospitalized with gunshot wounds. As a result of this traumatic experience, the board appointed an acting Superintendent until they were able to work through the chaos created by the murder of Dr. Foster.

Several months later, a new Superintendent was hired, and I decided I would begin "testing the waters" to determine if I could find a suitable district to run as Superintendent. At the time, there were few black or minority people holding that position in California. I knew that many of the "headhunters" frequently did not consider minorities unless the board specifically requested to see minority Superintendent candidates. As positions appeared, I applied and was submitted to several Boards of Education. I was selected in each case to be interviewed but was rejected from meeting the interview panel. I always felt they lacked the courage to hire a black candidate. My feeling was borne out when I met several board members who interviewed me and shared excellent feedback about me. After these experiences, I became somewhat discouraged, yet still personally motivated to pursue the position.

In seeking counseling and support from one of my graduate professors, he asked, "Have you applied for Sequoia School District?" He had shared with me earlier that the Superintendent there was retiring. I had forgotten the "tip"—and, most importantly, that he was conducting the search. He called the student personnel office and had my papers sent over to him, and I applied. And, as they say, the rest is history. This is how the search was handled. There were 80+ candidates who applied for the position. Those who were recommended were interviewed by two panels: one panel consisted of prominent citizens from the community, and the second panel was the board. I was the top choice of both panels. All the issues raised in the interview, I answered—I had landed the job!

MY FORMATIVE YEARS
DR. ELIZABETH H. REYNOLDS

I was born in the South in Memphis, Tennessee, in a family of nine children. I was told that my mother and father met in Mississippi and married at a young age. My family was a churchgoing, Missionary Baptist Church group. In addition to attending church every Sunday, of course, we paid our tithes and dues. On par with church, school was number two in the hierarchy of family expectations. In fact, we played school a lot. I specifically recall playing rock school at home and on the church steps.

My father stressed the value of education and how a good education would make us better. Before I was born, he had been a teacher in Grenada, Mississippi. You could teach back then without having a college degree. He had taught school and knew that education was important to him, and my parents instilled this value in all nine children. We all went to school and obeyed our teachers; we also obeyed our parents, and if not, of course, there were consequences because my father "did not play." My older brothers and sisters were born with the assistance of midwives in our home; I was the first child in our family born in a segregated hospital in Memphis. Our schools were also segregated during my time in elementary school, junior high school, and high school. I graduated from George Washington Carver High School in Memphis, and I do not recall having a white teacher until college.

Thinking back to grade school, I can recall my teachers having a lot of confidence in me. They motivated me and stated that I could do anything that I set my mind to. Consequently, I wanted to excel. I did not know what I wanted to be; however, I knew I wanted to be recognized for doing something good. This motivation on the part of my teachers, my parents, family, and church left me with no choice but to want to excel in whatever area I had deemed important for me. I decided to attend a junior college in Memphis. I also understood that I had to work while attending college, and along that same line, I was determined not to ask my parents for one single penny while attending college. After completing junior college, I knew it had been a great experience for me. It allowed me to mature and to make some decisions about where I wanted to go from there. At that point in my life, I transferred to the University of Arkansas at Pine Bluff. I decided to major in Elementary Education and was determined to land on my feet. I had found my niche. I loved teaching. I loved the children, and they loved me.

Before I graduated from my undergraduate program, recruiters from different places talked to me. When Kansas City, Missouri, came after me, I signed my first teaching contract. I thought I was rich! I was placed in a school as a young, black first-year teacher in a school with all white students, teaching second grade. This first year of teaching was the best I could ever have had. The parents loved me. I loved my students. That is when I realized that it does not matter how young you are or what color you are; a good teacher can teach all students anywhere.

I am bragging right now, in case you missed it. This first teaching job was an excellent experience, and I didn't want to leave. When I took maternity leave after two years to have my first child, I cried, the parents cried, and my students cried too. During my second year of teaching, I started graduate school. Over the next year, I completed my master's degree in elementary education at Kansas State University in Emporia, Kansas.

Because a distant relative knew about positions in Chattanooga, Tennessee, I was contacted and offered a position as a lead teacher in an elementary school. This was an offer that I decided I could not refuse, especially because returning to Tennessee would allow me to be closer to my relatives while working in the Chattanooga school district. Every three years or so, I was offered positions with additional responsibilities, opportunities, and pay raises. This was absolutely the place to be. I served in several roles in Chattanooga, from lead teacher, to supervisor, to grants director at the district office, to Elementary K-12 Director, to Executive Director, and finally Assistant Superintendent for Teaching and Learning at the Cabinet level. While moving up in my career, I was always in school pursuing advanced credits and degrees, taking classes at the local university, as well as classes from the University of Knoxville. I also worked as an adjunct professor at the University of Tennessee at Chattanooga.

I completed my Doctorate of Education degree from Vanderbilt University while still working as an Assistant Superintendent in Chattanooga. When I graduated from Vanderbilt, I was certified as a Superintendent for kindergarten through 12th grade. Working in Chattanooga, I had other opportunities to travel and make presentations to other school districts across the country. Additional accomplishments include being selected as a participant in Leadership Chattanooga, where I learned about the inner workings of the entire city of Chattanooga. Following that, I was selected to participate in Leadership Tennessee, where I had the opportunity to travel across the state and learn about the fundamentals of the state of Tennessee.

Other experiences for me included being selected as one of 50 educators to be a part of the State's Career Ladder Program (Pay for Performance Program). The National Superintendents' Prepared Program was one of the best experiences a Superintendent could have. The leadership sessions were held in different places across the country, with the trainers being the best leaders in the field of public education. The class included Superintendents from all over the country. These were sitting Superintendents who had served successfully in large urban school districts in places like New York, Detroit, and New Jersey. These were some of the highlights of my career, including being coached by my husband, Dr. Harry J. Reynolds, who had also served as Superintendent. After serving as Assistant Superintendent, I was interviewed by headhunters for an opportunity to serve in my first superintendency.

After my first interview for a Superintendent position, I was selected as one of the three contenders for the job in Spotsylvania, Virginia. While I was not thrilled with the job in that district, I felt that this was an excellent opportunity for me to go through the process and practice. Initially, I was afraid because I did not feel confident. As I thought about this opportunity, however, it dawned on me that I was fully prepared for the job. I made the short list! While I was not offered the slot, I felt confident that I interviewed well. In fact, I was coached and inspired by my husband, a seasoned Superintendent.

After attending an American Association of School Administrators (AASA) conference, I shared my experiences with several headhunters, and all of them seemed interested in hiring me. I had a choice to make: where did I want to live? The headhunters shared my portfolio; several districts started to call for follow-up interviews. Naturally, these were all national searches. Within a few weeks, the first district to respond was a district in Illinois; next, a district in New York, and then a district in North Carolina. The district in Illinois wanted to include my name in the national search, and I agreed. A total of about 120 individuals had applied; the board began their screening of applicants, down from 120 to 20 and then 10, and finally to the top three applicants. I was selected as one of the top three. The district arranged for me to fly to Illinois for my interview and become involved in the formal process. I was interviewed by several groups, including the teachers' union, parents, district office, community, and the board. After a lengthy process, I was offered a contract, and my life as a Superintendent began!

"A to Z"
Here We Go!

A

APPLY YOURSELF/ACKNOWLEDGE

A

Apply Yourself/Acknowledge

> *"In all thy ways acknowledge him, and he shall direct thy paths."* *(Proverbs 3:6 KJV)*

It is up to you to prepare yourself for duty by putting your best foot forward. In the position of Superintendent, your opportunities to create a great district are endless, and your opportunities to create a great team of colleagues are better than ever. Your learning curve is steep and becomes steeper as you become more engrossed in the position. While you will make mistakes as you grow in the position and become more familiar with the needs of the district, it is important that you apply yourself and become a quick learner. "Apply yourself" means to work hard at something, especially with a lot of intent, in order to complete a task successfully. The position of Superintendent can be compared to marriage. However, for some Superintendents, it may be better compared to a partnership that develops over a longer period of time. For some Superintendents, it seems like the marriage/partnership/relationship is over after several dates, or like the honeymoon is practically nonexistent.

There are many demands inherent in becoming an effective Superintendent. It is all about good leadership. Before becoming Superintendents, we began our careers as classroom teachers. We loved teaching, and both of us can still teach even today. Earlier on in our careers, we decided to teach, and we wanted to be the best teachers we could be. We wanted to be the kind of teacher that students always remembered because we brought out the best in them.

Our observation is that the most effective Superintendents have come from the ranks of effective principals and teachers, and they remain effective teachers in their new role. These individuals become leaders by demonstrating strong leadership traits early in their career, even as classroom teachers. As beginning teachers, they demonstrate a strong desire to master the skills necessary to move their students to higher levels of learning and create in their students an eagerness for learning. When these individuals become principals, they transfer the same knowledge and skills to the principalship with fascination and thirst for learning.

And now you want to be a Superintendent? A basic requirement is to maintain those excellent teaching skills. It is a necessity! Serving as Superintendent, you will have the opportunity to teach Boards of Education, principals, teachers, district staff, paraprofessionals, clerical staff, parents, community leaders, volunteers, and elected officials.

You must maintain those excellent teaching skills throughout your career. Serving as Superintendent involves teaching and leading your Board of Education. There will be many opportunities to teach and lead professional development sessions for your Board of Education, your community, and your staff. You are teaching and leading your Superintendent's Cabinet (the highest-level decision-makers in the school district) and your direct reports. You are teaching and leading your principals and key administrators in the district on a daily basis because they are watching you. You are also the main teacher and leader in all the teaching and learning initiatives. You may be the catalyst for many of the educational initiatives implemented throughout the district.

As a Superintendent, you must understand how to make new connections and maintain them. This provides you with a whole bucket full of resources and, believe me, you will need them. If you are serving in a suburban district, it is important to connect with other suburban Superintendents in order to keep abreast of common issues.

A

Elizabeth: In my second year as Superintendent, I was in Illinois, and my friend was in Minnesota. I was preparing to kick off the school year and needed a great motivational speech. My colleague stated that she had already written her keynote, and she had some ideas that she wanted to share. This is a great example of networking. I returned the favor to her and to others on several occasions. Another advantage was having a husband who is a Superintendent. Many times, when I had an event that was scheduled where I needed to speak, I would ask my husband to brainstorm several potential ideas with me. I would use my own framework, and he would assist me in "putting meat on the skeleton." I always wondered how my husband could speak without a note in hand. I understand now that it takes a lot of experience and confidence.

Confident communication as a superintendent grows from reading a variety of sources and building your knowledge and experience base. You cannot acquire any new knowledge without applying yourself. Through networking, a leader acquires much knowledge. By no means am I saying that the only way to succeed is to find you a Superintendent spouse! Networking locally, statewide, nationally, and even internationally is essential.

Because of the success we have had as Superintendents, we have been asked to lead many local, state, and national seminars at conferences such as NSBA (National School Boards Association) AASA (American Association of School Administrators) NMSA (National Middle School Association), CUBE (Council of Urban Boards of Education), and many state conferences, such as the Illinois Association of School Boards (Triple I conferences in Illinois), for over 15 consecutive years.

Some of the sessions that we have been involved in are:

- From the Board Room to the Classroom: High Expectations Produce Positive Results

- A Place to Call Home: Our New Teacher Network and Mentoring Program That Works

A

- PLCs (Professional Learning Communities): A Model of Excellence
- Exercising Accountability for Results: The School Board of Education's Role
- Creating and Sustaining a Successful PLC (Professional Learning Community)
- Enhancing Your Instructional Skills Through Differentiation in a PLC (Professional Learning Community)
- Linking Leadership with Student Achievement: A Collaborative Effort
- Don't Fuss Over the Small Stuff?
- Teaching and Learning: Classroom Strategies That Work
- A Trauma-Sensitive School District: Five Years Later

Our commitment to lifelong learning is paramount and has guided our practice as educational leaders. We never move away from the main thing—teaching and learning—and never forget why we entered the profession in the first place.

> **Elizabeth:** At the beginning of each school year, always the first week in August, I arrange a mandatory two to three-day retreat with all Cabinet-level staff. At the end of the school year, by June 1st, I provide them with some books or articles to read prior to our meeting, which is usually held at a remote site away from the district. This is my time to welcome them back and to spend time with them preparing to kick off the next school year. This event involves a lot of work on my part; however, it is well worth it. I am just as excited as they are. I always use great teaching tips and best practices in education. We review ground rules. I begin with a continental breakfast, including a large lunch and snacks, and we also take individual and group pictures. They work hard, and they are treated well. We have a lot of fun! Door prizes and an evaluation are provided at the end of the retreat. (*See next pages for sample agenda*)

A

ADMINISTRATIVE PROFESSIONAL
DEVELOPMENT MEETINGS

Thursday, August 1, 2019, 8:30 a.m. – 3:00 p.m.
Friday, August 2, 2019, 8:30 a.m. – 12:00 p.m.

Goals

- To increase the achievement of ALL students

- To close the achievement gap

Objectives

Participants will:

1. Know and understand the research on student achievement and instructional leadership.

2. Utilize data in a way that will lead to increased achievement of all students.

3. Schedule staff in a way that will increase achievement of all students.

THURSDAY, AUGUST 1, 2019

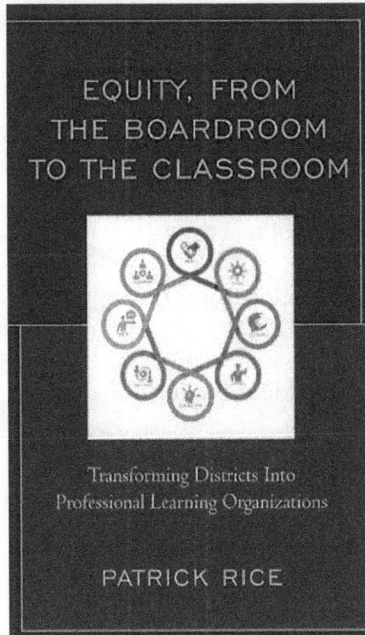

8:00 a.m.	Coffee and Treats	
8:30 a.m.	Ground Rules	
8:35 a.m.	Icebreaker/Team Building Activity	Speaker 1
9:00 a.m.	Welcome/Overview/Agenda/Purpose/ Expected Outcomes	Speaker 2
9:45 a.m.	Break	
10:00 a.m.	Professional Learning Organizations (PLO's)	Speaker 3
11:30 a.m.	Lunch	
12:30 p.m.	Presentations on Equity, From the Boardroom to the Classroom Why Organizational Culture Matters/ A Look at PLOs	Speaker 4

A

A Look at PLC Teams	Speaker 5
The Power of Informed Oversight and Systematic Governance	Speaker 6
Benefits of Becoming a PLO	Speaker 7
The Role of the Community Engagement Process	Speaker 8
Implementation Stages of Becoming a PLO	Speaker 9
School Board Leadership	Speaker 10
Final Reason Why Districts Should Choose to Become a PLO	Speaker 11
Concluding Thoughts	Speaker 12

2:15 p.m.   Wrap-up
Door Prizes

Language of Successful Managers

1. How can I help?
2. What do you think?
3. Your work matters.
4. I trust you and our team.
5. I appreciate your commitment.
6. Thank you for working hard.
7. I was wrong, I am sorry.
8. Your career path is my priority.
9. Do you have the tools for success?

FRIDAY, AUGUST 2, 2019

8:00 a.m.	Coffee and Treats	
8:30 a.m.	Icebreaker/Team Building Activity	Speaker 1
9:00 a.m.	Language of Successful Managers	Speaker 2
9:45 a.m.	Health Break	
10:00 a.m.	Updates and plans (any new initiatives you have planned) for the upcoming school year Department Managers	Speaker 3
		Speaker 4
		Speaker 5
		Speaker 6
	Principal	Speaker 7
	Business Office	Speaker 8
	Teaching and Learning	Speaker 9
	Safety	Speaker 10
	Buildings and Grounds	Speaker 11
	Human Resources	Speaker 12
	Parent Liaison	Speaker 13
11:15 a.m.	Lunch	
12:00 p.m.	Wrap-Up Questions/Answers Door Prize	Speaker 14

A

SCHOOL DISTRICT

Superintendent's Office

"High Expectations Produce Positive Results!"

August 2, 2019

Leadership Team Member:

I have full knowledge of the Board Policy Manual and Administrative Procedures for School District ----. I also have full knowledge of the Collective Bargaining Agreement (CBA). I understand the Superintendent's expectations for the 2019-2020 school year.

_____

Signature

_____

Date

WANT TO BE A SUPERINTENDENT?

WELCOME BACK
School District
Staff Institute
Day 1
School Building 1
AGENDA

Time	Activity	Group	Presenter(s)	Location
8:10 a.m.	Welcome	All Staff	Speaker 1	Gym
8:15 a.m.	Resilience Activities		Resilience Team	Room 101
	Why Try Training	Team 1	Why Try	Room 103
	School Improvement	SIP Team	Speaker 1	Library
	Technology Tools		Speaker 2	Room 108
	Safety Training	Safety Team	Speaker 3	Conf. Room
10:00 a.m.	Health Break			
10:15 a.m.	Resilience Activities		Resilience Team	Room 101
	Why Try Training	Team 2	Why Try	Room 103
	School Improvement	SIP Team	Speaker 1	Library
	Technology Tools		Speaker 2	Room 108
12:00 a.m.	Lunch	All Staff		
12:45 p.m.	Resilience Activities		Resilience Team	Room 101
	Why Try Training	Team 3	Why Try	Room 103
	Technology Tools		Speaker 2	Room 108
2:15 p.m.	Health Break			
2:30 p.m.	Wrap Up	All Staff		Gym

A

WELCOME BACK
School District
Staff Institute
Day 2
School Building 1
AGENDA

Time	Activity	Group	Presenter(s)	Location
8:10 a.m.	Welcome	All Staff	Speaker 1	Gym
8:35 a.m.	Ice Breaker	All Staff	Speaker 2	Gym
9:00 a.m.	PLO's	All Staff	Speaker 2	Gym
10:00 a.m.	Health Break	All Staff		
10:15 a.m.	School Resilience Activities	All Staff	School 1	Room 101
			School 2	Room 103
			School 3	Library 107
11:30 a.m.	Lunch			
12:15 p.m.	Data Disaggregation		Team Leaders	
			PreK-K	Room 101
			1st Grade	Room 103
			2nd Grade	Room 112
			3rd Grade	Room 114
			4th Grade	Room 110
			5th Grade	Room 109
			6th Grade	Library
1:45 p.m.	Health Break			
2:00 p.m.	Data Disaggregation		Same as above	

WELCOME BACK
School District
Staff Institute
Day 3
School Building 1
AGENDA

Time	Activity	Group	Presenter(s)	Location
8:10 a.m.	Welcome	All Staff	Speaker 1	Gym
8:40 a.m.	Ice Breaker	All Staff	PD Committee	Gym
9:00 a.m.	Staff Handbook	All Staff	Leadership Team	Gym
9:45 a.m.	Safety		Speaker 2	Gym
10:15 a.m.	Health Break	All Staff		
10:30 a.m.	P.B.I.S./SEL		Team Leaders	Room 101
	Planning			Room 103
				Library
11:30 a.m.	Lunch	All Staff		
12:15 p.m.	Team Time	All Staff	Principals	Room 101
				Room 103
				Library
1:30 p.m.	Health Break	All Staff		
1:45 p.m.		Team Time	Same as Above	

A | WANT TO BE A SUPERINTENDENT?

To become a Superintendent, you do not need 25 years of teaching. However, it is wise to have several years of successful classroom teaching before pursuing this position. The grade levels you have taught may not be as important as how successful you were as a teacher. Both of us found success as teachers at all levels, which resulted in advancements in whatever hierarchy we were in. The opportunities were endless because of the obvious impact we had on students. We were motivated.

> **Elizabeth:** Harry started teaching junior high school students and eventually continued to teach students up to the high school level. I started teaching in elementary schools (student taught in kindergarten) and eventually taught middle school, high school, and at the college and university level

Preparing to become a Superintendent takes time, effort, and real investment in continuing education. You should become knowledgeable about organizational management, budgeting and finance, human resource management, curriculum, instruction, parental and community involvement, and politics, to name a few. All are essential to learning how to become a Superintendent. No matter how fully prepared a candidate thinks he/she is, all the knowledge and preparation in the world does not substitute for being in the position of Superintendent. How a leader communicates and engages with the audience—that is, the Board of Education, teachers, parents, students, and the community—influences their response and your message more than any written words.

With each new challenge, we had the opportunity to gain experience in other aspects of our organization. It is important for developing leaders to adopt a growth-oriented mindset whereby they transfer skills in new roles. The same knowledge, skills, and abilities needed as an effective teacher are also needed as a Superintendent.

Some similar skills for both teacher and Superintendent include:

A

- Having high expectations for yourself and others

- Having a clear vision of excellence

- Having the ability to translate the vision into goals

- Commanding respect

- Creating order and a climate of peace

- Using time wisely

- Having standards of excellence for himself/herself and students for what he/she wants staff and students to know and be able to do

Having the ability to monitor and adjust those standards is critical. To be a great Superintendent, you must be a great teacher. Superintendents are super teachers. They teach principals, teachers, parents, students, and the broader community.

> **Elizabeth:** In my first job as Superintendent, because we were short on hiring substitute teachers, I decided to put my name on the substitute list. I also insisted on my principals doing so as well. After all, we were all certified. The purpose was three-fold: it allowed the district to save money, it allowed me to get into the school to see what was going on, and finally, it showed the teachers that I could still "get in the trenches" with them and teach. For some reason, from then on, we rarely needed substitutes during my time as Superintendent. At first, this concept was pretty shocking for principals. After some time, however, the principals found the opportunity to substitute, and they stated later that they rather enjoyed it. As a part of our strategic planning, I trained over 75 stakeholders using the Nominal Group Technique. This was an opportunity for me to use the knowledge and skills I had acquired in my early training in graduate school. This gave me a huge amount of validation with the community.

A Superintendents teach *teachers* how to teach by teaching principals how to lead. They teach them about academics and pedagogy. A Superintendent should conduct professional development sessions with principals and teachers at all grade levels. They are charged with creating an environment where their teams are well suited to lead instructional excellence. Superintendents employ their innovation and their access by engaging their staff and including community partners. They set the tempo and create the blueprint that amplifies the characteristics and the priorities of the district they lead.

> **Elizabeth:** In my first superintendency, I worked on curriculum mapping with groups of teachers at all grade levels, district-wide. This project covered the entire year. I was the lead teacher, I shared the research with the teachers, and I also taught them the process of curriculum mapping. I had to show them that I could teach them this process just as they would teach their students the process of reading or doing mathematics. While teaching all about curriculum mapping, I invited the high school administration and the high school teachers to join us, along with university professors. They were delighted to come to the table and were shocked to have this honor because they were never invited before. While teaching the teachers in my first district that I served, I always modeled excellent teaching habits in each professional development session that I led.
>
> As Superintendents, we must always model what we want from our principals and teachers. I wanted my principals and teachers to become master educators; hence, I was their master leader. I realized that I was being watched, and I had to stay on point!

An accomplished teacher is a teacher who feels confident in his/her career choice. An accomplished teacher is a person who, over the course of his/her career, has developed the necessary skills to successfully teach all children. This teacher is an avid reader and stays abreast of all the education research. The teacher has a strong knowledge of instruction and uses data to support his/her decision to move a student from one learning target to the next. The accomplished teacher does his/her homework and is perceived by his/her colleagues as a master teacher. These same traits are necessary for any Superintendent. Because principals are in a very critical role as the head of the school, Superintendents must teach principals and ensure they know what good teaching looks like.

> **Elizabeth:** My expectation for my principals has always been that they know how to teach. The principal must understand academic content and pedagogy. He/she must be knowledgeable of the standards, including what all students must know and be able to do. And the principal needs to know what to do if the students do not meet the standards. The principal cannot wait until assessment time. He/she must have a system that involves looking at formative data for each subject area, grade level, class, and student. There should be no surprises or knee-jerk reactions.

Accomplished Superintendents manage well. They are required to have strong management skills in order to lead a school district. A Superintendent should be able to go into any classroom and discriminate between an effective and ineffective teacher. Knowing the exact specifics of every subject matter taught across the school is not necessary. What is necessary is that the Superintendent must know whether the teacher is delivering quality instruction. In an interview for the position of Superintendent, you can be sure that one of the questions asked of you will focus on your proficiency in curriculum and instruction. A board member may ask the questions, "What are you specifically suggesting can be done instructionally to raise the performance of the 6th, 7th, and 8th-grade students in reading?" "What skills do they need to master, and what are the strategies of teachers to ensure students are successful?"

A

Harry: I started my teaching career in Richmond, California, as a teacher of social studies, American history, and biology. I had three preps (preparations), since I had three different subjects to prepare for. As a newcomer, I thought I could rely upon the veteran teachers as mentors. I soon discovered that many of them had developed routines that were radically different from my learning at the university. I student taught with a teacher who was pregnant, and because she was going to take maternity leave, I adopted skills from her that proved beneficial to me.

As a new teacher at De Anza High School in Richmond, California, I continued graduate work at San Francisco State University. I continued taking graduate classes in the area of counseling, which enriched my learning curve. I also had conversations with teachers who were willing to share their experiences with me. I continued in the learning mode as I moved from year to year. Over my six-year period of teaching at the high school, I learned that my favorite subject was biology. As I completed my master's degree in counseling during the six years of teaching, I moved into a counseling position (district-wide) in my seventh year.

I remained in counseling for a couple of years, during which I worked with junior high school youngsters who were having issues adjusting behaviorally with their teacher. Although I moved over into counseling after my sixth year of teaching, I had accomplished all my teaching goals during the six-year period. I felt like an accomplished teacher after my 15 years of service to that district. I came to school prepared and did my homework.

Additionally, since I taught both biology and social studies, I dropped by a packing house frequently on my route to school to get specimens for my 7th, 8th, and 10th-grade science classes. I also followed the practice of collecting specimens from the newspaper in order to share information about the civil rights movement. In order to enrich my students' experiences, I encouraged them to collect data articles from newspapers, television, and magazines.

This information enriched my classes as we discussed the civil rights movement and its impact on the world. Their items triggered powerful discussions in the classroom regarding the issues that were occurring nationally.

There is no substitute for the value a Superintendent brings to a district when he/she is an effective instructor. Instructional leadership is a pipe dream if the instructor does not have strong teaching skills. Superintendents take on the position to influence the direction of a school district. In order to do this, they must model and promote the importance of quality instruction. Apply yourself!

> **Elizabeth:** Serving as Superintendent in my third school district, I worked with staff and organized our New Teacher Network and mentoring program to recruit, retain, and train new teachers. This was not new to me, because I brought this idea with me from my work in Tennessee. We just made it better. It became so popular and effective that the teachers' union insisted on the program becoming a part of the contractual agreement. The union members included it in the language of their contract, and it became one of the highlights of the district because the teachers loved the program so much. From time to time, teachers are asked to write reflections about the program and to respond to the question, "What are the factors that motivate you to be a successful teacher?" (A sample reflection is provided on the following page.)

A

NEW TEACHERS' NETWORK
(SAMPLE AGENDA)
Monday, February 24, 2020
3:00-4:00 p.m.
Library - Room 107

AGENDA

1. Welcome

2. Good News

3. IAR Revisited (Tools and Practice Test)

4. Teacher Presentations (Reminder)

5. Classroom Management Ideas and Strategies (By Schools)

6. Evaluations

7. Door Prize

Quote for the Day

"Try to turn every situation, positive or

negative, into a learning experience."

– Vicki Caruana

Name: ████████████████   Position/ Grade Level: Kdg.

Years of Teaching: 33

What are the factors that motivate you to be a successful teacher?

I have a great love for working with children. This is one of my greatest gifts to teaching. In order for you to be successful you have to love what you do. I am a very dedicated and passionate person. My main focus is on academic achievement. My goal as a teacher is to give my students something the can take away and use for the rest of their lives. My mission is to ensure that all children learn. I give 100% of my time to my students. I consider myself to be an outstanding teacher because of the excellent classroom management skills and organizati. skills that I have, my commitment to education, and the love that I have for teaching. I am able to maintain a positive relationship with all administrators, teachers, coworkers, parents, and students. This is very important. The following characteristics describe the type of person I am. I am very dedicated hardworking, responsible, cooperative, dependable, understanding, punctual, very energetic, loving, caring, enthusiastic, and very committed to my teaching career. Although "High Expectations Produce Positive Results" is the theme for our School District 132, I have adopted this standard for myself and my students, and expect Positive Results.

A

Name: ███████████ Position/ Grade Level: kindergarten teacher

Years of Teaching: *this is year eleven*

What are the factors that motivate you to be a successful teacher?

One of the main factors that keeps me motivated is my belief that I am uniquely qualified to impact the lives of children and their families. I love all children unconditionally, and I know that not everyone ~~even~~ does. I have worked hard and searched long to learn to trust my ability to identify the needs of every student in the room. And I know that not everyone has done the same.

~~████~~ I believe that it is vital that we pass along to children the experience, and understanding that learning can be fun. Finally, I believe it is ~~our~~ my duty, and our duty, to create and maintain public education structures and experiences that ensure every student learns to problem solve and critically think in order to execute their Constitutional Rights. When we don't, we end up with a political and criminal justice system that does not serve our Democracy.

A

Name: ▮▮▮▮▮▮▮▮▮▮ Position/ Grade Level: Pre – K Blended (SPED)

Years of Teaching: 6

What are the factors that motivate you to be a successful teacher?

I am a successful teacher because I am invested in my students and their long term success. I am motivated by my love of learning and children. I am motivated by my students success whether big or small.

Name ▮▮▮▮▮▮▮▮ Position/ Grade Level: 2nd grade teacher

Years of Teaching: 5

What are the factors that motivate you to be a successful teacher?

The students -- I cannot let them down. They spend most of their week with me. I have to do and be better for them. I want them to realize their potential for future success, and that, in large part, depends on me. My students don't have the ability to control a lot of what happens in their lives at this point, but I can be a caring, reliable adult that has their best interests at heart

A

Name: ▮▮▮▮▮▮▮ Position/ Grade Level: _Adm/All_

Years of Teaching: _13_

What are the factors that motivate you to be a successful teacher?
What motivates me to be a successful teacher is knowing that I have made a positive impact on a student's life especially when students are craving for more knowledge and information. Secondly, I believe what motivates me to be a successful teacher is my passion to see every student learn and succeed because I believe that there is a "genius" ability in each and every student. Thirdly, seeing a student that had challenges when they were in school but seeing them become successful after they leave me. Fourthly, helping parents who appreciate my hard work and encourage me to continue what I'm doing with the students. Also, what motivates me to be a successful teacher is seeing the big grins on students' faces when they grasp a new concept that they thought was impossible and it becomes possible. Lastly, my daughter motivates me to be a successful teacher because the same academic expectation that I desire for her; is the same expectancy that I want to have for my students.

Name: ▮▮▮▮▮▮▮ Position/ Grade Level: _Teacher 1st gR_

Years of Teaching: _4_

What are the factors that motivate you to be a successful teacher?
The evidence that the strength or weakness of the academic foundation a teacher provides and the tone of the environment they manage can influence a student's belief in themselves and what they can achieve in life.

A

Name ██████████████ Position/ Grade Level: _Teacher/7th_

Years of Teaching: _____5_____

What are the factors that motivate you to be a successful teacher?

Being a teacher is one of the most challenging yet gratifying jobs you could have. My students inspire me to make them want to learn and to ensure that they look forward to coming to school each day. I work hard to try to reach each student and form relationships so that they know that I care and want them to succeed. Everyday is a new day and it is very rewarding to see my students progress in any way. I challenge my students to be the best person possible and to always do their best. I love teaching and coming to work each day at Calumet.

Name: _____ ██████ _____ Position/ Grade Level: _____

Years of Teaching: _____8 yrs._____

What are the factors that motivate you to be a successful teacher?

My motivation comes from seeing the growth of my students. I am also motivated to go even further when the students enjoy the lesson

A

Every Child is GIFTED.

They just unwrap their packages at different times.

*Dr. Elizabeth H. Reynolds with
students as they learn how to read the newspaper*

A

B

BELIEVE

B

Believe

> "*Jesus said unto him, if thou canst believe,*
> *all things are possible to him that believeth.*"
> *(Mark 9:23 KJV)*

A powerful prerequisite for any Superintendent candidate is the ability to communicate a solid belief system. Your set of beliefs about why you know you have the ability to do the job well influences your level of confidence. It enhances your desire to lead and direct large groups of people and groups of schools, and your hope to effect change for the benefit of the whole community. An effective Superintendent believes that all children are capable of learning at high levels and believes in his or her ability to move the district forward and propel students to high levels of learning.

Superintendents must prepare teachers to meet instructional goals. This means that they must be fully committed to preparing teachers to be successful, as none of the goals of the district and the expectations of the Board of Education and community can be met without highly committed and effective teachers. Superintendents must establish norms of high achievement for staff in working with students and counteracting apathy, negative attitudes, ineffective practices, and low expectations. The staff must be committed to producing high achievement for all students regardless of challenges, and a Superintendent must be committed to moving the district forward no matter what it takes (Wilbur Brookover, Creating Effective Schools, 1997).

If you are interested in becoming a Superintendent, you must direct all efforts to ensure that students learn at high levels. You must exude the assertiveness to get the job done and ensure that academic goals are met and students move to the next level. You must be prepared for the awesome task of making sure kids win! The self-fulling prophecy is evident. If Superintendents believe all students can learn at high levels, it is more than likely that students will meet those expectations, given the time, resources, and a set of caring and committed adults both in and outside of the schoolhouse. On the other hand, if the attitude of the leadership is one of defeat, even the most motivated child will fail.

Harry's Reflections:

I worked in California in two school districts for several years. I served in the role of teacher, counselor, dean, assistant principal, high school principal, and regional Superintendent. My career in the Richmond California Unified School District started as a science teacher at a high school, where I served for six years. Because I have a master's degree in counseling, I was asked to apply for an advertised counseling position in the district and was subsequently offered the job as a counselor at Portola Junior High School. I worked there for two years, after which I was assigned as a traveling counselor to five junior high schools in the district. My task was to visit each of these schools one day per week. Additionally, my responsibility was to deal with challenged students at the junior high level, who required more intense counseling.

Because I had certifications in counseling and administration, at the end of my tenure at DeAnza High School, I was told that I would be going to Kennedy High School as vice principal. I was still living and teaching in California at that time. In my role as vice principal, the principal assigned me responsibility for much of what was going on with the athletic programs and all aspects having to do with student affairs. After two years, the principal of my school was promoted to the district office as Deputy Superintendent. Because the Superintendent and the new Deputy Superintendent believed and had confidence in me, I was promoted to the principalship—which, by the way, the faculty also wanted me to do.

B

During my tenure at Kennedy High School, our school, of all the schools in the Bay Area, was free of disturbances among students. Our students were organized in such a way that student body officers stepped in and actively resolved areas where student conflict was evident. All of this was resolved by our students. I had been at Kennedy for several years when I was invited by the new Superintendent of Oakland School District to come in to see him. As you would know, he offered me a job as the Regional Superintendent in charge of one-third of the schools in Oakland, which comprised about 22,000 students that I would have responsibility for overseeing.

During the fall of that school year, as I embarked on my initial year as Regional Superintendent in Oakland, I also continued my graduate work. On one particular evening, a board meeting had been scheduled, and I had been excused, as I shared earlier. When I arrived home, I was informed that Dr. Mark Foster, Superintendent of the Oakland Public School District, and Dr. Robert Blackburn, his Deputy, had been shot as they were walking to their vehicle after the board meeting. Dr. Blackburn was struck but was able to run for cover; however, Dr. Foster was mortally wounded and did not survive the ambush. None of the assassins were identified by the Oakland Police at that juncture. Dr. Blackburn was hospitalized for several weeks for surgery and other restorative treatments. After several months, he returned to work until we were able to recruit a replacement for Dr. Foster. If you are wondering who the culprits were, they were the Symbionese Liberation Army. As you will note, this was several decades ago. However, it was an extremely disturbing experience for me, one that I will never forget.

Elizabeth's Reflections:

I also worked in two school districts as a teacher, lead teacher, **B** supervisor, assistant director, director, executive director, and assistant Superintendent before being offered a position of Superintendent. My first interview was with a school district in Virginia, and I landed the job. I was ecstatic! This was a great experience for me because I did not realize how intense the interview process could be, but I was prepared.

At least two things are occurring when you go out for an interview for a Superintendent's position. First, the Board of Education is trying to determine if there is a fit between you and the district. In other words, would they really like to hire you? Secondly, you (as the candidate) are trying to determine if you are interested in working for that district. Our goal has always been that we wanted to be fully prepared for the interview.

Believe in yourself! Having confidence in your ability is a requirement for the job. As a Superintendent, you must be confident, not cocky or arrogant, but BOLD! Believe in your potential to move a district forward. Know that you must be prepared to take on that responsibility. That is the expectation for accepting the position. If you are the candidate of choice for the board, then, because they respect you and will give you their support, you will be able to make positive changes that are evident rather quickly.

When I accepted my position as Superintendent in my third school district, there was a real opportunity for me to make several positive changes right away, because so many things needed to be repaired or changed. For example, the district was in such disarray that the state and the district entered into a governmental agreement that literally put the district under the supervision of the state for three consecutive years. I was serving as the District Superintendent, and the State Oversight Committee was working with me. This really

B

allowed me more leverage. I had two Boards of Education: my regular elected board and the Oversight Board of Education. There were two board meetings per month. Because I had experience as a seasoned Superintendent, I performed my duties as I would ordinarily perform them.

The oversight came into the district because the district was considered dysfunctional. The district had had several Superintendents, students were failing, the district was unclean, the budget was not balanced, the district lacked highly qualified teachers, the community lacked confidence in the district, and there were several lawsuits because of poor management. The Chamber of Commerce shared with me that they disrespected the district and would not support it because of the poor reputation it had gained. There had been a ton of negative articles in the newspaper about the district. You name it, and it was there. I made up my mind upon accepting the position that I would not fail. Failure was not ever a possibility. I felt that the training and the experiences that I acquired had prepared me for the position. I knew that *with God, all things are possible!*

Many times, plans are made with good intentions, and over time they fizzle out. "A good plan gets you in the game, but executing your plan gets you into the winner circle." (Lee J. Colan, *Sticking To It: The Art of Adherence: How to Consistently Execute Your Plans,* 2003).

Elizabeth: You must believe in yourself and your ability to get things done. If you are like me, you always want things done yesterday. I have learned that patience is good. While you believe that you can turn a district around, with belief comes a plan of action: both a long-range plan and a short-range plan. They are equally important. Furthermore you have a vision and mission statement, and you know what you want to see happen, you have ideas.

Superintendents in a broken district (e.g., problems in student achievement, finances, human resources, professional development, teaching and learning, safety) must contend with negative community perceptions along with internal and external strife. Time is often not on their side because years of neglect result in impatient board expectations in the face of enduring conflicts and limited resources.

In a district such as this, seasoned superintendents with a track record of reform and success are most poised to change a failing district to a successful district by addressing the key issues that threaten its success. Some districts may be so dysfunctional that it would take "an act of God to change it, but a broken district is an opportunity to make a huge difference in the life of the community.

We have had the opportunity to work in districts such as these. We looked at it this way—"the only way to go is up." Our route to success in districts that were broken took an act of God, belief in God, and a focus not on ourselves but rather on the best strategy to meet the goals. We specifically identified the most important matters, and progress monitored incremental change. God was the co-pilot, and we were the pilots. We had to have a strong belief system. Otherwise, we felt that we would not have been able to do the hard work of turning a failing district around. We had to believe we were capable of doing the job that seemed impossible. It was complicated, difficult, and seemingly insurmountable—not for the timid.

B

Maywood schools tackle reform

By Diane Rado
Tribune staff reporter

With six of its 10 elementary schools labeled as failing last week—the worst showing in the state outside Chicago—the Maywood-Melrose Park-Broadview school district finds itself in upheaval, frantically trying to convince students that they shouldn't flee.

An outspoken new superintendent, who started on the job July 1, has already replaced two principals at failing schools and rushed into a controversial overhaul of curriculum.

And for the first time in at least a decade, the district plans to charge registration fees to help pay for its academic reforms, which include school on Saturdays for struggling students.

The roller-coaster ride has left administrators, teachers and parents reeling. As many as 150 parents walked out of a school board meeting last week, surprised and upset over the new registration fees this fall, which will cost $30 for the first student and $10 for other students in a family.

But Supt. Elizabeth Reynolds isn't deterred.

"Time is not on our side," she said. "We've got to go with what we know right now, something that will jump-start this district."

It is one of the most dramatic examples of the plight struggling school systems face, especially as federal reforms bear down on them. The state's announcement that 232

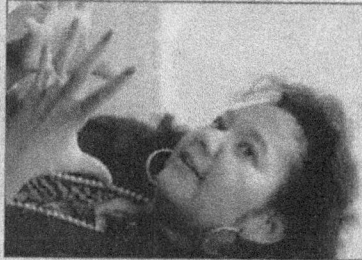

PLEASE SEE **DISTRICT,** PAGE 6

Photo for the Tribune by Peter Thompson
Supt. Elizabeth Reynolds

B

YOUR LOCAL SOURCE • $1.00

MELROSE PARK
HERALD

WITH NEWS OF STONE PARK
A PIONEER PRESS PUBLICATION

August 7, 2002

www.pioneerlocal.com

District 89 Superintendent
Elizabeth Reynolds speaks
to administrators and
teachers about improving
the district.
Page 3

NEWS

Drug Treatment Court
sees numbers rise.
Page 5

SCHOOLS

Triton classes are for the
ages.
Page 13

DIVERSIONS

A group of Tibetan
Buddhist monks will
perform sacred music.
Page B3

SEE SECTION C FOR
CLASSIFIED ADVERTISING

Inside!
Education
Guide

B

C

COURAGE

Courage

C

> *"Be strong and of good courage, do not fear*
> *nor be afraid of them; for the LORD your God,*
> *He is the One who goes with you.*
> *He will not leave you nor forsake you."*
> *(Deuteronomy 31:6 NKJV)*

Courage is the inner drive to make progress regardless of the difficulty. For every person, there comes a time when you must step forward and meet the needs of the time. Regardless of whether your moment is now or sometime in the future, you must be ready. When you move forward, even through the path of most resistance, you gain the courage necessary to win.

> *"Courage is contagious. When a brave man takes a*
> *stand, the spines of others are often stiffened."*
> —*Billy Graham*

> *"Whatever you do, you need courage."*
> —*Ralph Waldo Emerson*

Changing a school district that has been managed ineffectively for years is not an easy task. A leader who seeks change will often meet with resistance. A Superintendent, before considering stepping up to the role in a beleaguered district, should ask difficult questions of the recruiters or board members who conduct the initial discussions. Extensive research is beneficial prior to making the decision or accepting the slot, so they should position themselves to find out as much as they need to find out about the district.

In making a decision to accept a troubled district, one must bring to the table a successful history of managing and turning around a district of this sort. When you know that you have been offered the position as Superintendent of a troubled district, then you must bring to that position your successful experiences as well as the courage you displayed in managing and turning around a district. Because it will be necessary to make a change, you must be certain the change is well thought out. Change just for the sake of making change is nonsense. Change should never be done in a piecemeal fashion.

To accomplish total change in a positive research-based fashion, you need to accept the fact that change happens systematically and incrementally. True change is systemic, and it impacts every aspect of the school and/or school district. As a leader, you must put in place the policies, procedures, materials, and supplies necessary to accomplish your goal of making positive change. Courageous leadership is needed at all levels of the organization. Every leader has to become passionate about the change.

ALWAYS HAVE THE COURAGE TO SPEAK THE TRUTH

In the course of advertising for a Superintendent position, most districts make clear the qualities they are seeking in a successful candidate. If the desired qualities are not obvious in the advertisement, the qualities will usually become apparent during the interviewing process. The wise candidate keeps track of this kind of input and its source as an indicator for further discussion with the board.

Sometimes the board reveals in an interview its concern about incompetence or bad decision making when it occurs among principals. They inquire as to what a Superintendent would do to rectify the situation. In answering this question, the candidate must be sharp enough to explain exactly what will be done to deal with this situation. The candidate must also be diligent in identifying what problems exist and making sure the exact action steps are evident in both long-term and short-term plans. It is important for the board to know that you are aware of problem areas and that you are responsive with prompt, well-thought-out solutions.

Harry's Reflections:

<u>Turn-around Tips</u>

In nearly all of my administrative assignments, I have had to deal with ineffective personnel. Many of these situations existed because someone before me did not have the courage to do the job or thought more highly of the needs of the adults than the children.

As a master teacher and administrator, the Superintendent needs to know what is transpiring in a school. Some information may come through subordinates; however, it is good for the Superintendent to visit the schools to see how the education process is going. A Superintendent visit does not mean a visit to the principal's office.

Over the course of my career, I have learned many lessons that have allowed me to get to know the district quicker and to generate better plans for systematically moving the district. One such practice is to become familiar with certain documents:

- Academic trend data
- Budget reports
- Required fiscal audits
- Personnel records/evaluations

- Expenditure reports/Standard Operating Procedures

- Attendance data for students and staff

- CBA (Collective Bargaining Agreements)

- Health/life safety audits

- Board of Education policy book

In addition to regular visits to classrooms, I monitor data that reflect how various aspects of the organization are processing Superintendents' work to create effective schools. If you are selected to serve a district that has all blue-ribbon schools, great, this is rare. Even still, your job would be to have courage, and to make certain you maintain the same reputation and image needed to keep the "blue-ribbon" status, as that would be the expectation of the Board of Education.

Elizabeth's Reflections:

If the district you have been selected to serve is not performing well, then the Board of Education is usually looking for a person who has the wherewithal to change the district or "turn the district around." Many districts look for "turn around" educators or, as the late Dr. Asa Hilliard would call them, "Barrier Busters." These individuals have gone into districts that have several problems and been successful in turning the district around. Now, this cannot be done in a year. It usually takes three to five years or more to turn a district around.

Turn-around Tips

I was asked to accept the charge of turning a district around when I arrived. The district was plagued with every problem possible:

- Dysfunctional Board of Education

- Ineffective teachers and schools (no focused teaching)

C

- Poor achievement
- Outdated technology
- Unclean buildings
- Unbalanced budget
- Union and administration conflict
- Long list of union grievances
- Lack of compliance in the special education program
- Lack of compliance in the bilingual program
- Grant funds were frozen because of lack of follow-up
- Large number of unqualified staff
- Lack of professional development plan
- Low community perception image
- Lack of parent/community involvement
- Staff lacked materials and supplies
- No long- or short-range plan
- No strategic plan
- No evaluation system for staff (certified and non-certified)
- Large number of lawsuits
- Large number of substitute teachers
- No Board of Education/Superintendent goals or objectives
- Outdated Board of Education/District policies and administrative procedures

- Lengthy and unproductive Board of Education meetings

- In-home fighting among Board of Education members

C

Where do you start?

Communicate with your Board of Education and community about the district commitment first. Brief your Board of Education. Effective communication is critical. That means constant communication with the Board of Education, principals, administration staff, district office, parents, community, and all stakeholders.

I communicated on a daily and weekly basis via email, or as a document with reminders and updates (which I refer to as my Weekly Board of Education Update), on a monthly basis at Board of Education meetings, and on a yearly basis at my State of District Progress Report meeting and my Parent Orientations at the beginning of the school year. I also communicated through half-day Data-Driven Teacher Professional Development Sessions, spoke at each monthly Chamber of Commerce meeting, and contributed to quarterly Community Newsletters. Everything that was mentioned was sent out, turned around, or fixed within a few months to a year.

OPENING YOUR BOOK?

It takes courage to step out into this arena, the Superintendent's arena, where you are sharing your skills and experiences—you become an open book. The Board of Education looks carefully into your life in order to decide if you have the profile they would like to lead the district/community. If you are asked to be interviewed by the Board of Education, it takes courage on your part because you are also making a decision as to whether you are prepared to do well in your interview and land the job. You are consenting to be under a magnifying glass. Your private self becomes public domain because you are a servant of the community.

C

A challenging yet essential aspect of the role of Superintendent is navigating the interests of both parents and teachers. The critical success of the district lies in how students and families perceive their schools and the level of academic success that is realized. Highly effective teachers with high morale drive this success. But when children aren't learning and parents aren't pleased, no matter how happy teachers may appear, the equilibrium is off. Success-oriented teachers feel less empowered, and morale suffers. Superintendents are always trying to keep the climate one of effective output. Maintaining a highly functioning organization requires a Superintendent to consistently check the pulse on an ongoing basis through progress monitoring and communication with all stakeholders.

"Courage is about having the guts, nerve, and heart to do things that foster and support progress. And that begins with the realization that: 1) improvement won't be found on the path of least resistance known as conformity, and 2) status quo is the archenemy of progress. When you think about it, "doing things the way we've always done them" requires no leadership at all. What is there to lead to? How can others follow someone who's not going anywhere? That's why 'leadership' and 'courage' must be viewed as synonymous concepts" (David Cottrell and Eric Lee Harvey, Leadership Courage: Leadership Strategies for Individual and Organizational Success, 2004).

"Courageous leaders avoid the temptation to fix blame and focus on the past. They opt, instead, to focus their attention on the future … on ways to solve situations as they are. If you have the courage to take blame words out of your vocabulary and accept responsibility to move forward, there's a good chance that your team will follow your lead. When that happens, everyone wins. To become a courageous leader, you must realize that accepting responsibility is not optional—it is mandatory. Accepting responsibility leads to confidence, self-control, and trust. And those are all qualities of effective leadership" (Cottrell and Harvey, 2004). Effective leadership ensures an effective superintendency.

Harry's Reflections:

<u>Collective Bargaining</u>

Years ago, many school district teachers gained the right to bargain collectively (labor unions). I believe the model adopted (industrial) was not proper for education—and its most adverse impacts were on urban districts. While it helped to correct the improper behavior of some administrators, it did not improve a lot of urban black and non-European students. The major concern I have is that, in some districts, there is no representation for urban and poor children at the table. Many bargaining agreements that have been signed have not been in the best interest of children. Many agreements have been written to protect incompetent teachers, with some educators who may "talk on both sides of their mouth" knowing that these incompetent educators they are protecting will never teach the children of the wealthy and powerful, but are more likely to end up in urban schools.

The person who aspires to lead a school or district needs to be committed to every child being taught by the most dedicated and competent people available, and if a teacher cannot do the job, no child will be exposed to that person. The right of all children to have a competent teacher is greater than that of an incompetent teacher to have a job at the expense of a powerless student. No educational leader should protect or maintain an incompetent staff at the expense of poor children for whom he/she should be the active voice.

<u>Case:</u>

In my first assignment as superintendent, I met with the representative of the bargaining committee on a regular basis (monthly). The purpose of the meetings was to discuss any issue about which either side was concerned and which we wished to communicate and resolve. Early on in my career as a Superintendent, there were complaints about why one teacher was not carrying the class load set forth in the contract.

C

After several meetings, I visited the school and this teacher's classes. I entered the classroom with the sound of the first bell, greeted the teacher, and sat at the rear of the room. When the second bell or starting bell rang, there were only about ten students present and ready to work. This was the way the day progressed. After the last class was dismissed, I asked the teacher where his students were. He replied, "This is all who signed up for the class." He added that he rarely gained more students, and some dropped his class over the course of the semester. I thought to myself, "Oh!" At this school, students chose their classes as they do in college. Students above the freshman level, or those who know the students and teachers, deliberately avoided him. They avoided him for as much as three years before finding a place in a class where there was a good teacher.

The principal knew of this problem and avoided it because he did not have the courage to act, and he was removed. This is a case where the union would have been supportive of the principal. Unions are usually very supportive when an administrator has followed all steps in the CBA (Collective Bargaining Agreement). A bad teacher gives good teachers a bad name. Lacking the courage to proceed and handle a problem is one of the worst things a leader can do. Everyone's watching to see what the leader will do. No action means you are condoning the problem. You either take steps to resolve problems, or you become tagged as the creator of problems. Not good!

MASTERING THE
LEADERSHIP ATTITUDE

A poor leader...

C

1. Makes extensive use of cynicism and sarcasm
2. Frequently uses words like "adequate" and "status quo"
3. Is negative and defensive
4. Has an apologetic manner
5. Is a "buck-passer"
6. Is known as a procrastinator
7. Is intolerant and abrasive
8. Makes simple things seem complex
9. Has a poor personal image
10. Often seems in a quandary – lacks sense of direction
11. Often given to self-pity
12. Plays favorites
13. Has an aura of tension and nervousness
14. Is unpredictable
15. Is seldom punctual
16. Garbles communication
17. Has low sensitivity to needs of co-workers
18. Sets poor example in dress
19. Is known for pessimism
20. Practices "scapegoate-ism"
21. Is disorganized
22. Frequently shows anger
23. Has little sense of humor
24. Is afraid to "rock the boat"
25. Does not know the research

C

WINTER 2020 / ISSUE 16

BEHIND THE SCENES
CALUMET PUBLIC SCHOOL DISTRICT 132 NEWSLETTER

Superintendent Dr. Elizabeth H. Reynolds... speaking during New Staff Orientation

WELCOME BACK EVERYONE!
Superintendent Dr. Elizabeth H. Reynolds

NEW YEAR, NEW GOALS!-

...A look back at the first half of the school year

Now that year 2020 is here, we must continue to strive and move forward by providing an interesting and exciting learning environment for our students. According to an African Proverb, "It takes a village to raise a child," so let's work together to create that peaceful and nurturing village for our students! If our students see that their teachers and parents are united, then they will feel more supported and more likely to make better decisions.

I encourage parents to remember that setting aside time to assist your children is an important requirement. Assisting them with their homework and getting them involved with extra curricular activities will help increase their abilities to do well academically and socially! We are looking forward to a brighter New Year accomplishing New Goals!

D

DESIRE

Desire

> "Delight yourself in the LORD, and
>
> he will give you the desires of your heart."
>
> (Psalm 37:4 ESV)

Many educational leaders have a sense of longing for the position of Superintendent. It is the pinnacle position in K-12 educational leadership. When there is a vacancy in a district, even if there is a staff member in that district who is next in line for the position, there will usually still be a national search. Sometimes an individual's desire will exceed their demonstrated ability and preparation. Frequently the person who is assumed to be the in-house competition is really not the best person to make the changes needed in the district. Sometimes the in-house person is busy trying to line up votes from their favorite Board of Education members rather than ensuring that he/she has the necessary qualifications if offered the job.

In order to realize and recognize the right fit, you must start with a strong desire to perform the job of Superintendent well. The mindset you bring to the job is extremely important for your success. If you feel that you are capable of doing the job, then have a positive attitude about it, along with a sense of grit towards it. This means you must be ready for the smooth sailing and the rough ride. We realize that being a Superintendent is a phenomenal job. Many people want the job, but having gained the job does not mean wanting to do the hard work that is involved in keeping the job. When you get the job, you are working from the knowledge base that you acquired from your educational experiences and graduate school. Look the part. Act the part.

There are many D words and phrases that we can think of, such as: DEMAND excellence of yourself and everyone else. DO your homework on all issues, including when you are preparing for the interview and when you are offered the position. In preparing for the interview, conduct a mini-research study on the district. If the district is in your state or area, drive around and ask questions of parents and business owners. If the district is not near you, make it your business to physically visit the area and talk to as many people as possible. Seek out news articles and online sources that will keep you abreast of the history of the community, its climate, and its education. Read, read, and read! The more research, the better. After you have done all of your research, you may determine what questions to ask and what specific clauses to put in your contract. Further, you may be able to forecast what questions may be asked of you, and you will have a scope on what the community needs.

DEALING WITH DIVISION
—A FORMER SUPERINTENDENT REFLECTS

The Superintendent's experience is dichotomous in terms of its scope. In one sense, a Superintendent is expected to be a decision-maker, leading the execution of educational improvement and guiding its direction. In another sense, the authority Superintendents are thought to have may be in superficial, dysfunctional environments. In that case, the Superintendent is merely a decision-maker, relegated to carrying out the actions others have made, regardless of the intent of those decisions. As a public servant, the Superintendent is a keeper of the will of the community, but the challenge and disappointment comes when a community is misguided by public or political opinion and unaware that they are sowing seeds of their own destruction. For a passionate change agent leader, this dynamic is debilitating and silences the voices most prepared to create the change needed in that community. The right that the Superintendent seeks to propel is distorted in the wrong, because petty power dynamics resent leadership and block progress. This deems a Superintendent immobile, which debilitates the role, rendering the leader unable to do the good work on behalf of the community that they came to do. Great leaders seek novel ideas. Poor leaders work alone. Bad leaders hate change and won't take risks.

D

Harry's Reflections:

Definitely Dazzle

We advise candidates about what they should know and do to improve their chances of being selected or considered. Look at the requirements and experience in the description of the position: what is the district looking for?

We remind would-be Superintendents of the importance of your image and appearance. There are communities where the appearance of the Superintendent is an important reflection of the board and the community. As a chief educator, we need to present in all aspects the knowledge, image, and climate that reflects the institution. If you are the leader, you should know, look like, smell like, act like an example of a super master teacher.

Finally, be comfortable with yourself and the image you are portraying. As Superintendent, people are really watching you.

Watch these behaviors:

- Appearance
- Chews gum on the job and in front of constituents (exhibiting poor manners)
- Is a sloppy dresser
- Has a hygiene problem
- Does not comb hair

- Has unclean fingernails

- Has worn, unpolished shoes

- Wears excessive makeup

- Smells of cigarette smoke

- Has body odor, resulting in complaints from constituents

- Appears unprofessional, is a gossip

- Fails to take pride in appearance

- Does not groom facial hair

- Ignores requests to improve appearance

- Does not carry self with confidence

- Is always disheveled

- Underdresses for professional meetings

- Projects a negative image of the company

- Is uninviting, people request to be seated away from this person

- Eats with mouth open

- Is lacking in manners and appropriate social conduct

(Anne Bruce, *Perfect Phrases for Documenting Employee Performance Problems*, 2005)

D

PARK FOREST

Bringing Local News Home

NO. 49

AN EDITION OF THE STAR

SUNDAY, DECEMBER 14, 1997   50 CENTS PER COPY

96 years of Local News

06/14/98   P   103730
BD OF ED SCHOOL DIST 163
242 S ORCHARD DR
PARK FOREST IL 60466

Reynolds shaking up Dist. 163

By Leah Berenholz

Park Forest-Chicago Heights School District 163 is actively responding to three October community forums that sent a clear message to staff and faculty that academic standards and achievement are the community's prime concern for its schools.

Public information coordinator Denise Paris said the forums were unprecedented in the district and were a first

Reynolds

Continued from Page A-1

to make analyses, compare and contrast, and defend their points of view rather than just answer yes and no questions."

Reynolds also started several programs to get the students more excited about reaching academic achievement goals.

She began the principal's word of the day program, which introduces students throughout the district to one new vocabulary word each day. Teachers define the word for students and then ask them to use it in a sentence. Reynolds also drops in on classes and asks students to spontaneously define and use one of the principal's words.

step in creating a long range plan for improvement.

One of the first responses to the forum results has been an effort to audit the curriculum in various departments and make necessary improvements.

Faculty from the district as well as high school and university representatives are involved in the curriculum analysis, Reynolds said.

"We are looking at the gaps and the

some classrooms to test children on their multiplication tables through multiples of 12. Her goal, she said, is to have all students know their tables through 12 by the end of the third grade.

Discipline standards and maintaining a positive school environment was also a top concern expressed by the forum participants, which included parents, teachers, university professors and involved citizens.

A committee formed two weeks ago will evaluate the district's current discipline policies and suggest changes. The final code of conduct will be made available to students and parents.

"If we don't have a discipline program that works we'll have one that works by the end of the year," Reynolds said.

Now that district leaders have

repetitions. We want to develop academic standards for pre-kindergarten through 8th grade," Reynolds said.

She said the math curriculum audit is finished and a science curriculum evaluation is now beginning.

In January teachers will participate in teaching workshops based on Mortimer Adler's teaching philosophy.

Adler's philosophy is based on the premise that the best instruction should

challenges they face, Reynolds said getting parents involved is necessary for success.

Reynolds led one workshop to teach parents how they can better help their children with math homework without purchasing the tools available to teachers. She said she plans to lead other workshops to teach parents how to motivate their children.

"Now that we know we have a lot of hard work to do (the staff) has been mostly cooperative and they see that we have a plan," Reynolds said, adding that she is pleased with the district's accomplishments since July.

"I'm not at all pleased with our achievement levels. We've all got to make sure we change the direction of the learning curve here and put it in an upward

be provided to all students, not just the best students. The teaching techniques Adler advocates include interactive lectures and response from students, supervised practice of lessons and high level questioning rather than rote memory questions.

"It allows students to do higher levels of thinking by teaching from art, a story, etc.," Reynolds said.

■ See REYNOLDS, Page A-4

E

ETHICS

*"Don't allow your moral
compass to ever take a
sabbatical."*

—Elizabeth H. Reynolds

Ethics

> *"And whatever you do, whether in word or deed, do it all in the name of the Lord Jesus, giving thanks to God the Father through him."*
>
> *(Colossians 3:17 NIV)*

Ethical Leadership is about how to judge what's right and what's wrong. And more importantly; how to do what's right. How do we judge what the right actions are? Antiracism? Gender discrimination? Covid-19 and discrimination? As well as safety with certain races? These are issues that are necessary for the health of a school district.

Act with integrity, fairness, and in an ethical manner. A good Superintendent leads by example and is ethical, trustworthy, and professional. The individual is firm, fair, and consistent; follows Board of Education policy; maintains transparent and honest relationships with the Board of Education; and communicates regularly with the Board of Education.

There is always value in having self-imposed values; they should guide you. We must learn to live out our set convictions. People know right away what we are about—our walk and talk must match as leader. We must blend our vision and mission goals into daily practice. We must examine ourselves and see if we have some deeply held convictions. As the saying goes, "we must stand for something, or we will fall for anything."

Our behavior must connect to our beliefs, values, and goals. As I (Elizabeth) talk to young parents who are attempting to understand what school is about, many of them will come to school for the first school meeting of the year, but will not return unless there is a problem. This is not good. I share with them that what they do speaks louder than what they say. This example reminds me of the many parents who are actively involved in their child's school. These parents attend the first meeting and also make themselves available for other meetings and events held by the school.

Visiting the school is not a one-item event. Parents are their child's first and most important teacher; therefore, the parents should be actively involved through the school year. This shows the child the importance of schooling. These parents are walking the talk. We must understand "how our actions either support or contradict our messages." "When you walk like you talk, you get the results you want.... Words to live by are just words unless you live by them" (Eric L. Harvey and Alexander Lucia, Walk the Talk: And Get the Results You Want, 1995).

When we do not produce what we have agreed to produce, or when we promise to do something but do not deliver our words, then what we say becomes a joke. It becomes meaningless. In my evaluation of one of my principals, the man was rated poorly in the area of ethics. I had previously discussed with him the commitments that he had been making to students; however, there was never any follow-through. He would ask students to read a certain number of books, and if they met that goal, he promised a pizza party at the end of the month. It never happened. Again, the principal asked the students to have their parents attend a special program, and the class with the most parents attending would have a pizza party. It never happened. The students became discouraged. This was embarrassing for the district because the principal's promise became a joke to the school. The word got out about the principal. Bottom line, if you can't do it, don't say it. Children hear what we say. More importantly, they watch what we do.

As leaders, we all come with a lot of labels. Some are true and some are false.

When you are selected as the candidate of choice for the new Superintendent, your first order of business is to get to know all aspects of the district as quickly as possible. Several effective strategies may be employed to accomplish this goal. Among them is to conduct a thorough audit on the district. We are about the business of educating children, so what you want to do is determine how effective the delivery of instruction is for all children, i.e., do all students have easy access to the most effective teachers?

In many cases, the practice of tracking has caused many poor and powerless students to be denied the most powerful teachers. The parents of these children often have to fight the administration in order to guarantee equal access to the best teachers, materials, supplies, and classes. Not only are the children denied access to the best teachers, but they are also denied access to interesting electives that may be able to stimulate them and make the education process more interesting. Sometimes, we have the responsibility to change the process by reeducating the faculty and the community.

Until all children have access to the best that we can offer, our district is not doing its job. This must be a long-term goal for all Superintendents. This may require a change in the way students are assigned, or it may call for changes in our board policies with board approval in order to move away from tracking. In fact, the first part of the process may involve having dialogue with the Board of Education to educate them and the broader community. When you get involved in initiating your strategic plan, these equity and tracking concerns will surface as a part of the long-range plan. There must be a deliberate goal including organized discussions and an implementation plan.

A second aspect of this auditing idea is that the Superintendent must set aside time to visit all the subsets of the school district (e.g., maintenance, cafeteria, etc.). Be out and about visiting schools during the time students are eating. Get feedback about the food. Find out what they like or dislike. Ask questions!

Some of these audits may be delegated to key staff members. However, it is crucial that you have firsthand knowledge of what is going on around the district. The Superintendent is leading a very complex **E** organization. The well-functioning ability of all the component parts is essential to achieving the main goal. It is important that each of these various groups are effective in supporting the main goal of the school district.

Equity means we are trying to provide for children who are poor an environment that is similar to or as good as that of affluent children. We want to show and tell our students that they are important. One concern of mine is never to allow any school to be unclean. This is an expectation that I have that not only are our schools safe, but we must have extremely clean schools. Teaching by example means that, for instance, if I see any paper on the floor in a classroom, hallway, or outside, I pick it up. This sends a strong message. If we expect greatness from students, rightfully, the students should expect greatness from their schools.

It is important to tell all staff who perform their jobs well how exceptional they are. There can be a day set aside for staff appreciation so the students can recognize them, custodians and clerical staff included. Bottom line, everybody matters and should be recognized for doing an exceptional job. We must recognize that excellence requires a commitment to equity.

A major concern facing the person who is in leadership at the principal or Superintendent level is the need to guarantee that all children have equal access to the best assets available in the school or district. This denial occurs most often in the secondary schools that actively practice academic tracking. The new Superintendent candidate entering a district and visiting a secondary school may find this procedure deeply rooted despite the research advising against it. Typically, students are grouped into classes according to standardized test scores or academic grades in a prerequisite course. Unfortunately, most of the lower-level classes are taught by the least experienced, least well-trained, and least effective teachers on the faculty. When the least powerful students are denied access to those teachers who have demonstrated the most success with students who have difficulty, it results in the neediest students being assigned to the least able teachers.

The Superintendent must always see him or herself as the advocate and protector of all students, the one who ensures that all students have equal access to the best that is available in the school. His or her job is to figure out how to make this happen.

The Superintendent must ensure that equity happens in all buildings, in addition to providing the necessary support. The Superintendent must actively visit schools and classes—yes, visit classes over the course of each school year. He or she must be known as the "walk around" Superintendent.

You must make it your business to visit the whole array of teachers, including those who are known to be "hot shots" and those who are known to be substandard. We must admit that we have some who are struggling. This needs to be clear in a Superintendent's mind when he/she goes in for the interview for superintendency. One of the interview questions may involve the issue of how to ensure equity in all schools for all children.

In the case of Illinois, Ralph Martire and Ed Condon ("An Unlikely Journey Toward Equity," The Journal of School Business Management, 2017) state:

While outside the profession many confuse "equity" with being "equal," practitioners have always understood that an "equitable" education means one that meets the specific needs of the students being served—and those needs never have been, nor will be, "equal." To date, the evidence makes it clear Illinois has largely struggled to provide an "equitable" educational experience to all students. According to data from the Illinois State Board of Education (ISBE), not only are there meaningful achievement gaps by race and income in Illinois, but there is also a material overlap between schools with **E** significant low-income and significant minority populations....

Fortunately, the winds of change—positive change—are blowing. With the enactment of SB1947—which implements the Evidence Based Model (EBM) of school funding, Illinois now has a school funding formula that's designed to provide every district the resources it needs to educate the students it serves. Which is great. However, actually getting state-based education funding up to adequate levels will take some time, given the EBM shows Illinois' overall investment in K-12 education is over $6 billion short of what the evidence indicates is necessary, and state government has an accumulated deficit in excess of $15 billion in its General Fund. That means school districts will have to find ways to cope with the legacy of Illinois' historically inequitable education funding system for at least the next few years, until such time as the state's fiscal issues are mostly resolved and the EBM is fully funded.

Due to the state's education funding shortcomings, most of the concern about issues involving equity in educational opportunity in Illinois has focused on school districts that serve a disproportionately high number of disadvantaged students—read that as low-income and/or minority students—to educate. Little of the equity discussion has involved districts which already have adequate resources to educate the children they serve, because their students generally tend to be high performing overall, and not, for the most part, either low-income or minority.

We believe in equity and inclusivity for all. We will ensure that every student feels empowered to achieve to his or her full potential, commit to provide equitable opportunities for all learners, grow an inclusive school community, and demonstrate we value diversity.

Mission Document - Sample

E In pursuit of academic excellence, our mission is to form a partnership with family, community, and the educational staff to develop academic, social, physical, emotional, and cultural needs of all students.

Our Educators Will:

Teach a standards-based curriculum and provide diverse learning experiences that meet the academic, social, physical, emotional, and cultural needs of all students.

We resolve to provide students with a **supportive environment** that is safe, respectful, and responsible.

Academically, we will promote the development of literate, motivated, and independent-thinking problem solvers.

Socially, we will promote the development of responsible citizens who are honest, kind, tolerant, and empathetic.

Physically and emotionally, we will promote the idea of learning to maintain a healthy and productive lifestyle.

Culturally, we will promote respect of cultural diversity, diverse opinions, others, and self.

F

Fearless

> *"But now, this is what the Lord says—*
>
> *he who created you, Jacob,*
>
> *he who formed you, Israel:*
>
> *"Do not fear, for I have redeemed you;*
>
> *I have summoned you by name; you are mine.*
>
> *Isaiah 43:1*

You must have a strong vision of what you want to do in a school district based on data and have the courage to act on the vision in order to accomplish your goals. It is essential to articulate the vision and to sell the vision (why you must get this done, and what difference it is going to make). Your willingness and strong desire to do whatever is necessary to sell and justify the direction is critical in order to get people on board. If you are running out there and you do not have the people running with you, then you are running alone. A "willy-nilly" approach about what you are going to do is not wise.

Being fearless is not a negative quality. Being fearless means that you boldly state your position about children and learning and your expectations and commitment to educating all children. When working with groups of individuals, you are still inclined to consider all sides of the issues and patiently work with those who may not personally be on board but are moving and willing to consider positions that may enhance the proposal or make it acceptable to a broader part of the population without losing the basic intent. Never give up on a good idea. You work with guys who may have different ideas about how to get something done. Don't squash them. Please look at their rationale, their "whats" and "whys."

Suppose you have been studying the adoption and implementation of a new math curriculum in the upper elementary grades. You are approaching the projected time for implementation, but a significant number of elementary teachers are still unsure about it. The teachers are not sure of themselves and unsure of the program. There are all kinds of grumbling among some of the teachers about things that are not relevant to the real issue. The Superintendent needs to be fearless enough yet patient enough to briefly delay the implementation until the real issues can be identified and resolved. This includes eliminating some dissenters whose real reasons may not be stated, yet should be valued.

As a leader, you must be strong enough to accept the fact that the best-laid plans may not work the way you want. You must learn to be flexible. You cannot say, "I don't care! You are going to do what I say!" You cannot have the "it's my way or the highway" attitude. We have seen and talked to some Superintendents who have had that mentality. Most of them have been short-lived Superintendents.

Harry's Reflections:

In one school district, we were starting to build a central data processing system with IBM modular mainframes (you can tell this was many years ago). You could increase the processing power (the computing power) by adding additional modules. Initially, we purchased enough modules to accommodate those schools that had been aggressive in coming up to speed, using the system they had. My most forward-thinking principals pushed me to come up with the money to add as many components as I could, since many of them had their data processing people work way beyond their assigned hours to find time to do their processing.

As more schools became proficient, the demand for more modules or time to compute grew, which made it essential to make some significant budget changes that were not anticipated. We sacrificed buying other district items in order to add modules to the mainframe at a more rapid pace. As a Superintendent, I had to make a tough decision based on a priority that was number one.

F

Fearless means getting back up and fighting for what you want over and over again, even though every time you've tried before, you've lost. Fearless is having doubts and moving forward in spite of those things that scare you to death. I have had a desire to assist educators who are committed. I have also left behind "hot-headed people," those who are fiery and seem to be impatient listeners.

Being fearless also means going after Superintendent positions even if you feel that you might not get chosen for whatever reason. When I have applied for an open Superintendent position, the racial makeup of the children is not an issue. I feel good about my schooling (not to brag), my experiences, and my training. I have always felt that I had the personal integrity needed to offer my very best—so I applied for the job if I met the requirements.

Over my career, I have been interviewed for the "top spot" and known that the individual who got the position was not as qualified or experienced. I continued to apply because I believed there was a position out there in a school district where the board would be thrilled to offer me a position.

This is where the scriptures come into play. Since I am a Christian, I knew that God was in control, and I felt that God knew what was best, even if I didn't. All things work out for the good of those who love the Lord and are called according to his purpose (Romans 8:28).

Dr. Harry J. Reynolds, with Board Members and Principals

Dr. Harry J. Reynolds, with Community and Business Leaders

Elizabeth's Reflections:

After years of serving as Superintendent, it became clear to me that being fearless was a part of the job. The thing that comes to mind for me is the school board election. In Illinois, there is an opportunity for community residents to run for a seat on an elected school board, which happens about every four years. These elections can become rather fierce. This could mean that the board that voted you in as Superintendent could change to become a board that wants you out. Some Superintendents become involved in the election and take sides, but this is something a good Superintendent never does. Even if the team that voted you in wants you to take sides, you cannot, because you never know how the election will end. My style has always been to stay positive during the election and remain fearless and prayerful.

From personal experience, when I accepted my first job as Superintendent in Illinois, it felt like the best job ever! Everything was moving so fast. It felt like the scenario where you're "feeding the baby and drying her at the same time." After my fifth year in that district, I felt that I had accomplished so much in a short period of time, and I thought I had accomplished all of my goals for the district. The district was in great shape both academically and financially. I did not have to leave; however, I felt like I needed a new challenge. I was asked to move to a larger district and duplicate the same turnaround success that I was blessed to have had for the five years in my first district. The same attitude, skills, and abilities are needed in a Superintendent's job, no matter the size. A reputation of success can be gained when you continue to operate at the same high level, no matter where you are. Again, my sounding board and my shoulder to cry on has always been my husband. Every issue that I approached, my husband had already dealt with, and he had the prior knowledge needed because he had already served as Superintendent several years before me. I felt so blessed.

As I reflect, I know that God had things all figured out for me. At one point, I was asked to accept a position in a smaller district. (One note to remember: do not put your focus on the size of the district. There are so many other things that are much more important, like the probability of success.) This district was in dire need of a seasoned Superintendent to turn it around. It seemed that this district was the "armpit" of the county. This small school district was in "intensive care" or on "life support." There was an issue in every area of the district, from academics to finances. I was invited to come to the district, and in spite of the horrible reputation it had gotten, I looked at this as an opportunity. This district would require oversight from the state for three years. I understood all of the issues and was determined not only to revive the district but to bring it to a place where we were being watched by the state not because of concerns but because of the excellence. Thank God this has occurred. We are being asked to present every year at so many different major local and national conferences.

This was an example of me being fearless. Getting myself together and picking myself up. Getting back in the game. Talking to myself, saying I know I have a lot that I can offer a school district as Superintendent if I am given an opportunity. You can say that to yourself over and over again. It does not hurt.

When you accept a position as Superintendent, you are offered a contract. The Board of Education conducts evaluations of you, usually yearly. You want the board to evaluate you so that you can have a document in writing that reflects your success in the district. On the other hand, if the board fails to complete your yearly evaluation, then your contract automatically renews itself. When you are confident you are delivering on your promise by improving the district, the board will usually offer you a multi-year contract, which can run for three to five years. When the board is really pleased with your performance, a five-year contract is almost always offered. In

Illinois, when you are offered a multi-year contract, you must have Superintendent Long-Range Goals (see the next page for a sample copy) that you will accomplish for the duration of the contract. We have been fortunate to have multi-year contracts offered after each of our first positions as Superintendents.

Being fearless means being confident, wise, and discerning. I am reminded of a time when several senior staff reported to me about a concern with my second-in-command person. The Cabinet members reported to me that this individual was rude to them and other staff, had a demeaning attitude, had intentionally put down other colleagues, and was disrespectful to teachers, administrators, and other staff members. Even the Board of Education members had heard complaints. I had an obligation to call a meeting with this individual and confront this situation. After much listening and discussion, I shared with this individual that I had to follow the policy, including the complaint process outlined in the School Board of Education Policy. I had an obligation to follow our Ground Rules generated at the beginning of each school year. The Ground Rules are originated by Cabinet staff and must be adhered to by all Cabinet members.

When there is a performance issue at hand in the form of a complaint, it must be addressed. As Superintendent, you have an obligation to address the concern. It does not matter if the accused has been a friend of yours or not. It must be acted upon! Your reputation is on the line. This is one of the most painful parts of the job as a Superintendent. In order to build a fearless reputation of respect and trust, you cannot sit on a problem or turn your head. It must be handled in a prompt and professional manner. We must get HR involved immediately. In summary, staff members appreciate Superintendents who are fair, consistent, and prompt. This builds strong relationships and certainly boosts morale.

The Basic Principles on which Future Action is Based:

If you want your team to be effective, you must have "Ground Rules."

F

GROUND RULES

1. All work must be focused on Student Achievement

2. Once a decision is made as a team, it stays

3. Listen to what everyone has to say without retribution

4. Respecting everyone's responses and time/begin and end on time

5. Conflict is handled in an atmosphere that does not lead to hostility or resentment.

**These Ground Rules are the framework and rules that are made to be honored!!

SUPERINTENDENT'S PERFORMANCE GOALS
SAMPLE

Goal I. The Superintendent will provide leadership necessary for all students within the district to improve total performance as measured by NWEA-Northwest Evaluation Association (or similar standardized testing program in effect at the district), data from the previous year, or meeting, or exceeding performance as measured against the national average of student performance from the previous year.

> Performance Indicators. The Superintendent will provide: (1) curriculum improvements, (2) training programs for teachers in the subject areas, and (3) an ongoing and thorough student improvement assessment program.

Goal II. The Superintendent will ensure the district is in compliance annually with all requirements for English Language Learners. The Superintendent will ensure the district is in compliance with all State and Federal rules and regulations for Special Education.

> Performance Indicators. The Superintendent will provide training activities for teachers and administrators in order to remain in compliance.

Goal III. The Superintendent will provide leadership to integrate technology with the district curriculum.

> Performance Indicators. The Superintendent will provide: (1) curriculum improvements which implement technology into the classroom, (2) training programs for teachers in the use of technology in the classroom, and (3) an assessment of the use of technology in the classroom to further the district's curriculum.

Goal IV. The Superintendent will provide leadership to maintaining a strong enrichment program that offers various activities for the students of the school district to participate in.

Performance Indicators. The Superintendent will provide: (1) an assessment of the present level of enrichment activities available to students in the district, (2) recommendations to improve, enhance and maintain student enrichment activities at all grade levels, and (3) and assessment of progress toward this goal.

Goal V. The Superintendent will develop a clear and concise expenditure plan to ensure effective and efficient use of resources for student learning. The Superintendent will ensure actual expenditures do not exceed budgeted amounts without knowledge and approval from the Board of Education.

Performance Indicators. The Superintendent will work with staff to maintain a wise spending plan.

Goal VI. The Superintendent shall provide leadership to evaluate the buildings in the district and to assess needed repairs or improvements, all in an attempt to provide safe facilities in a wholesome education environment for all students.

Performance Indicators. The Superintendent will provide: (1) a comprehensive recommendation for facility improvements, including bringing and keeping the district in compliance with health/life safety requirements, and (2) recommendations for sources of funding for building improvements.

Miscellaneous issues may also be addressed.

BOARD OF EDUCATION / SUPERINTENDENT GOALS
SAMPLE

Goal I
Strengthen curriculum and instruction based on identified needs to improve achievement of all students.

F 1. Continue school reform planning

2. Analyze achievement data district-wide and by school

3. Use specific action plans to address deficiencies at each school

4. Use academic standards for what students will know and be able to do Pre-K – 8 (More course electives)

5. Continue curriculum map as a means of auditing the curriculum

6. Continue professional development in areas where indicated to address staff capacity and other areas of need.

> - Improve pedagogical skills
> - Improve academic capacity

7. Develop long range technology plan (eBooks, tablets, etc.)

8. Provide equal access to uniform resources, textbooks, materials, supplies

9. Resources for Parents, Equity for Students

10. Working in collaboration with medical professionals to better service our students

Goal II
Strengthen and enhance the role of school site administrators.

1. Continue staff development activities to enhance leadership skills

2. Develop a training program for interested administrators designed to prepare educators for the future

3. Continue administrators in developing school improvement plans

4. Continue administrators in prioritizing needs for instructional improvement

Goal III
Improve student support services.

1. Continue to initiate, strengthen, and enhance the delivery of pro-active student support services

2. Redefine and expand role for social workers to better identify and serve the needs of students and families

3. Monitor and evaluate each school's Behavior Management Plan (PBIS - Positive Behavioral Intervention and Support)

4. Study Special Education and Bilingual programs in terms of demographics of population and quality of program, in order that students are served consistently (Bring into compliance areas of deficiency) in both programs (get outside assistance as needed).

Goal IV
Establish and maintain a recruitment, hiring, training and retention program in order that the most highly qualified staff is available to all students.

1. Continue early recruitment and retention program for certified and non-certified employees

2. Continue New Teacher Network and mentoring program

3. Initiate professional development program for all certified, non-certified and substitute staff

4. Create opportunities for staff to complete additional endorsements and degrees

5. Continue after school programs to reinforce student growth

F

Goal V
Develop a clear and concise spending and financial reporting plan to provide effective and efficient use of resources for student learning.

1. Continue a systematic process for allocating resources based on priorities

2. Review flow of papers and authorizing signatures required to determine "hang up points" and inefficiencies

> * Establish timely procedures
> * Provide more efficient service

3. Continue a fiscal audit which includes audit of functions and processes

> i.e.: (telephone usage audit)
> * Done legally
> * Checks and Balances
> * Ensure accountability
> * Establish written procedures

4. Continue appropriate organizational structure and staffing needed to efficiently support instruction

5. Continue systems for controlling expenditures

6. Continue budget development process which details how the budget is formed and how resources are allocated according to district priorities/and deadlines

7. Recoup any outstanding funds owed to the District

8. Maintain Balanced Budget

9. Maintain facilities and establish plan of action for new facility

Goal VI
Strengthen relationships at all levels within school district and with the community.

1. Continue to study school district and community needs and systematically develop long range plan for greater community involvement/communication

2. Continue to conduct community forums and focus groups as a means of getting direct input from parents and other stakeholders

3. Continue surveys with Board of Education, Administrators, Teachers, Support Staff, Parents and Community Leaders as a means of gaining insights/perspectives from their point of view

Goal VII
Improve Board organization, effectiveness and efficiency as a policy making body.

1. Maintain district School Board Policy Books/create Procedures Manual

2. Continue on-going board development and dialogue with Illinois Association of School Boards

3. Continue work with Board of Education to establish goals and objectives for District

Approved at October 16, 2016 Regular Board Meeting

WANT TO BE A SUPERINTENDENT?

F

| Wednesday, August 7, 2002 | MELROSE PARK | 3 |

Your Local

NEWS

In crisis mode

Dist. 89 leaders put forth plan for improvement

By JOHN HUSTON
STAFF WRITER

A packed house of parents came to hear Maywood-Melrose Park School District 89's plan to increase academic achievement.

Instead of a feisty crowd like the one that stormed out during a July 17 board meeting, audience members listened last week to administrators who presented their strategies for improving one of the state's statistically worst school districts.

"The purpose of this forum is to inform you, the community, of the nature and magnitude of the crisis in District 89," said Superintendent Elizabeth Reynolds at the July 30 assembly. "Most of our students are consistently performing under their grade level. We're in a crisis."

Her plan includes focusing on three areas in order to improve student performance: using effective programs, using effective processes to implement the programs and building capacity in the people who execute the programs.

Goals laid out

Reynolds laid out goals for the district, such as offering a foreign language beginning in third grade and requiring eighth-graders to master algebra before entering high school.

Another goal was met with skepticism by some parents in the audience.

"Our expectation is to have kids reading in kindergarten," Reynolds said. "We will not have kids making it to third and fourth grades not reading."

She defended the hiring of JP Associates, a New York-based consulting firm that specializes in a direct instruc-

tion curriculum aimed at increasing student performance.

The group will give monthly assessments of teachers based on student-achievement data, a move that angered many of the district's instructors.

"We need to get (teachers) the most help possible," Reynolds said. "Tiger Woods is a master golfer, but he still needs a coach."

In order to reach out to parents, the district will hold forums at all 10 schools during September to address problems specific to each site.

Karen Eisenbart, the district's new director of grants, outlined the district's scores on the 2001 Illinois Student Achievement and Terra Nova tests.

Most of the district's stu-

dents are below state standards on both tests.

Listed

Six of the district's 10 school are on the state's Academic Warning List, down from eight last year, she noted.

Eisenbart said that although four of the district's schools are not on the warning list, they will be required to show academic improvements just like the others.

In fact, the four schools not on the list are near the cut-off line, with each of them with nearly 40 percent of students below standards.

"All schools are expected to make progress," Eisenbart said.

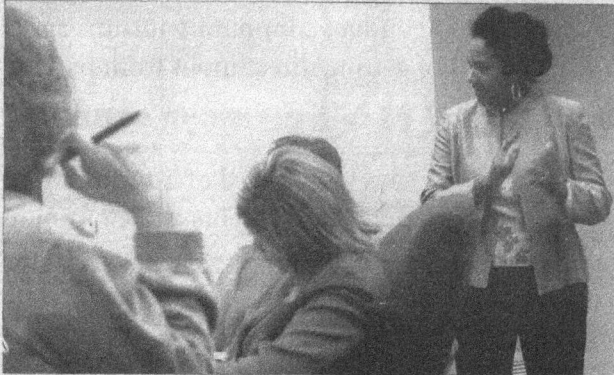

Superintendent Elizabeth Reynolds speaks to administrators during a three-day session aimed at improving the district.

Assistant Superintendent Connie Hoffman speaks about improving the school system.

Melrose Park Herald (USPS 903-590) Vol. 22, No. 30. Published weekly by Pioneer Newspapers Inc., 1140 Lake, Oak Park IL 60301. Single copy 51.00. Periodicals postage paid at Oak Park IL 60301 and additional mailing offices. One-year subscription $19.95. In county only. Call (847) 486-9300 to subscribe. Postmaster: Send address changes to Melrose Park Herald, c/o Pioneer Newspapers Inc., 3701 West Lake Ave., Glenview IL 60025.

SOUTI

CALUMET PARK

Panel to watch over schools

Oversight board members come with experience

By Kati Phillips
Staff writer

The board appointed to oversee a troubled Calumet Park school district includes a financial consultant with experience saving a bankrupt district.

Robert Grossi, the Bloom Township school treasurer since 1986, is among the seven members of the board that will meet for the first time Thursday to create long-term plans to improve programs, finances, buildings and staff at Calumet Park School District 132.

Grossi has served as the chief executive officer for the state-appointed school finance authority at Hazel Crest School District 152½ since 2002 and brought a problem-ridden audit to the attention of school leaders at the Sauk Village district, prompting a criminal investigation.

"I am looking forward to working with

Grossi

School District 132 and the Lincoln Park Zoo. Williams was a teacher, coordinator and director of special education for the Chicago Public Schools between 1969 and 2004 and now trains special-education teachers in a DePaul University program.

The other oversight board members are:

■ Kevin Burns, superintendent of Community High School District 218, the high school district into which District 132 feeds. He is the high school district's designee.

■ Joe Gatrell, a teacher in District 132 since 1994 and publisher/editor of the Blue Island Sun Newspaper from 1997 to 2003. He was appointed by the district's teachers union.

■ Marlene Talaski, an assistant professor at Dominican University in River Forest and a former public school teacher and principal. She was appointed by Calumet Park Mayor Buster Porch.

■ Alfreida Jamison, an eighth-grade math teacher in Robbins and teacher in District 132 from 1997 to 2003. She was appointed by state Rep. Bob Rita (D-Blue Island).

■ Deborah Beasley, an employee of the Blue Island Public Library for more than 20 years. She is the manager of children's services and is the appointee of state Rep. Will Davis (D-Hazel Crest).

District 132 has been on probationary status because of mismanagement since 2000 and nearly had its state and federal funding withheld at the end of last school year because its special-education program had so many problems.

The school board voted 5 to 1 in June to enter into an intergovernmental agreement with the Illinois State Board of Education providing for the oversight board.

The agreement expires June 30, 2008, unless the state board of education decides it needs to authorize extensions through 2011. The term can be extended beyond that if both parties agree.

Kati Phillips may be reached at kphillips@dailysouthtown.com or (708) 633-5976.

103

F

READY FOR SCHOOL?

Making 'tremendous strides'

Troubled Calumet Park school district progresses with help of state watchdog

By Kati Phillips
Staff writer

The first time a state watchdog met with Calumet Park school district's superintendent, the atmosphere was tense, to say the least.

Monitor Gary Lieder said he felt like he was carrying a club, and Supt. Elizabeth Reynolds probably felt like she was going to be beaten up.

But since that day in May, the two have developed a rapport more like Oprah and Gayle than Punch and Judy.

During the first meeting of the district's oversight board last week, Lieder and Reynolds volleyed back and forth, describing the progress made in troubled District 132 over the summer.

The goal is to maintain this harmony as new school staff improves day-to-day operations and the oversight board institutes long-term plans.

"Tremendous strides have been made, but there is still a long way to go," said Jonathan Furr, a lawyer for the state board of education who presided Thursday over the oversight board meeting.

"It is critical moving forward that this continues as a partnership," he added.

Calumet School District 132 has been on probation since 2000 because of mismanagement. Its most serious shortcomings were in special education.

Three state compliance reviews since 2004 showed expenditures were not being tracked, staff were unqualified and students were not being served.

State officials did not believe the district could fix the systemic problems by itself. They asked the school board to accept an oversight board and state-appointed administrators through at least June 30, 2008.

In June of this year, the school board agreed. The seven-member oversight board met for the first time Aug. 10 to assign point people for school board training, special education compliance, finances, instruction, staffing and facilities.

Lieder and Reynolds assured the oversight board that progress already has begun. For example:

■ The district has hired three new building principals and a new administrative team to direct finances, student achievement, human resources, grants and special education.

■ The business manager recoded the last fiscal year's expenditures so officials could track grant purchases.

■ The district identified 46 students who required initial special education evaluation or re-evaluation. All of the students will be evaluated before the start of school.

■ Three staff members from the Eisenhower special education cooperative reviewed all special education files. They flagged missing components and made sure student placements were appropriate.

■ The district held a staff recruitment fair on three separate days during the last week of July. More than 40 candidates attended, and 10 certified teachers were hired.

About two dozen parents, staff members, teachers, former teachers and school board members attended the meeting Thursday to see how the oversight board and school officials worked together.

The union president welcomed the oversight board, while two former teachers asked that the gifted program and aides be brought back to the schools.

Board member Janice Harrison criticized the oversight board for its composition.

Only two of its seven voting members are black, though the district's students are 82 percent black, 16 percent Hispanic and less than 1 percent white. A white teacher was appointed to represent the union without a membership vote.

Furr said race was irrelevant. It was up to the union to determine how to choose a representative.

Kati Phillips may be reached at kphillips@dailysouthtown.com or (708) 633-5976.

G

GROWTH

Growth

> *"But grow in grace, and in the knowledge*
>
> *of our Lord and Savior Jesus Christ. To him*
>
> *be glory both now and forever."*
>
> *(2 Peter 3:18 KJV)*

G

The school Superintendent has an extremely complex position, the ultimate job that most top educational public school leaders long for. This is the only job in the school district that directly reports to the Board of Education. The ideal Superintendent not only interviews well, the candidate must also value and understand the importance of personal growth. There are many advantages and joys of serving as Superintendent. You are looked up to by many groups of individuals: the board that hired you, the administrators, the teachers, students, parents, and the community. On the other hand, you are also faced with many challenges and critics. It comes with the job!

There was a study done in Illinois titled: "What does the ideal Superintendent candidate look like?" Among the traits determined in an ethical Superintendent, one was that the individual "maintains the standards and seeks to improve the effectiveness of the profession through research and continuing professional development" (Dean Romano, Illinois School Board Journal, March/April 2019).

Many times, Superintendents are hired in positions and can get so bogged down in crisis situations that the person does not carve out time to refresh, retool, or reboot themselves. This individual is headed for disaster. This person cannot continue to operate using the same old materials, skills, knowledge base, and credentials. As leaders, we must be open to new ideas and new ways of thinking. Superintendents must constantly be thinking, reading, and discussing new areas of interest in order to stay on the cutting edge of research. An effective Superintendent is a researcher and practitioner. A Superintendent must maintain a ready network of colleagues from across the country whom he/she can call on at any date and time for anything. For example, there may be a question about anything ranging from instructional issues to construction issues, and the instructional issues will vary widely.

G

A Superintendent needs to deepen and broaden his/her knowledge of the different aspects of the district that he/she is serving, and the profession itself. Again, this also involves creating relationships. Becoming a genius at networking is also an extremely important growth opportunity for any Superintendent.

Harry's Reflections:

During the latter period of my career, I had the opportunity to substitute for a teacher in a town 40 miles south of my home. The task required me to drive through the heart of an area where corn and soybeans were the major crops grown. Each spring, I derived great pleasure from observing the uniform rows of small plants peeking through the rich black loam to the point that bare corn or beans were ready to harvest. Observing this natural process always reminded me of the exciting 40-plus years I had given to nurturing countless boys and girls from pre-pubescent youths to highly productive citizens.

As I considered developing young educators to lead future school districts, I understood that they must have the ability to grow quickly. Successful candidates must be quick and hungry learners, able to discriminate between what is relevant and valuable for what he/she is trying to accomplish and what is a waste of time.

I have served six school districts, and all of them have had challenges that needed to be addressed. Because of all of the opportunities I have had to grow as a professional, I always felt prepared to face those challenges. In Sequoia School District, the population of individuals, the Board of Education, and the feeder or partner schools were the best of all of my experiences as Superintendent. If you ask me why that is the case, the reasons are many: The Board of Education was a group of strong professionals, as were the faculty and staff, and all groups were interested in promoting excellence for all children. All of the groups went beyond the call of duty to promote the welfare of every single student. The district was composed of predominantly two-career affluent couples, an upper middle-class district with mostly college-trained professionals. Working there forced me to be prepared, so I took on the task of personally growing myself. There was no way that I could float my way through. One thing was for sure: growth was critical.

G

Vanderbilt University Graduation

Berkley University Graduation

WANT TO BE A SUPERINTENDENT?

G

ADVISORY COMMITTEE FORMED — These are memers of the executive committee of the Hamilton County Association for Children with Learning Disabilities.

Fromeft ae, seated, Sharon Brown, of Ooltewah Middle ichol; Marilyn Smith, of the Hamilton County choes; Elizabeth Gaines, superintendent of elementary education in the city schools; standing, Dr. Earl Davis, of UTC; Reed White, of Rehabilitation Services for the State of Tennessee; Dr. David Dzik, optometrist, and Dr. Roger Meyer, clinical psychologist with Brainerd Psychological Services. (Staff photo by Robin Rudd)

A local look at **education**

Educators ready students for new century
Elementary schools key on improved technology, new programs

By Lynda J. Hemmerling

It's summer and school is out, but local school district officials already are gearing up for the next academic year.

Students may be spending their days swimming at a pool, running through a sprinkler, playing ball or lounging in the shade.

School superintendents and staff, however, are swimming through piles of paper, running through ideas for next year and probably not getting to lounge very much.

Improved technology, new programs and increased security are some of the items that will highlight academic 1999-2000 in school districts in Chicago Ridge, Frankfort, Hazel Crest, Orland, South Holland, and communities throughout the south suburbs.

In fact, Elizabeth Reynolds, superintendent of Park Forest-Chicago Heights School District 163, said there are new guidelines that school districts are expected to incorporate for the next millennium.

"There are 16 characteristics of schools and school systems for the 21st Century," Reynolds said.

"We are working on incorporating all of them, as are school districts across the country," she said.

All of the points are important, according to the Council of 21, American Association of School Administrators.

"The definitions of schools and students as learners are changing because of technology," Reynolds said. "In fact the digital world is creating the change."

Superintendent Douglas

Hamilton, of South Holland School District 151, said his district will be implementing a looping program at its four grade centers next year.

"We've always been a fairly innovative district," Hamilton said. "We've identified where changes need to be made and adapted to meet those changes."

■ See NEW, Page 76

G

New

Continued from Page 74

Hamilton explained that the looping program involves a teacher teaching a student for two grades in a row, while in the same grade center.

For example, a student who has Ms. Smith for kindergarten would also have her in first grade.

Then information about that particular student's grades, behavior patterns and academic learning style would be passed onto the teacher who would have the student for second grade and third grade, and so on.

Taft School houses kindergarten through first grade; Eisenhower School, second and third grades; Madison School, fourth and fifth grades, and Coolidge Middle School for six, seventh and eighth grades.

The looping program at the district's learning centers helps "bond parents, teachers and students together," Hamilton said.

Additionally, there would be more of a social and emotional tie between a teacher and a student.

Academically, teachers would have a better handle on students' academic learning styles and have more time to "get to know" students and how best to educate them.

"The idea is that we're creating more of a sense of family," Hamilton said.

Prairie-Hills School District 144 is also aiming for a more cohesive feel.

As of July 1, J. Kay Giles signed a long-term contract for five years to be superintendent of schools.

Giles, who has worked in the district for 20 years, has been superintendent for three years.

Through Giles' efforts, Prairie-Hills was awarded a 21st Century Community Learning Grant to establish an after school program for students in collaboration with community sponsors.

The district — which serves portions of Country Club Hills, Hazel Crest, Markham and Oak Forest — also has been awarded numerous technology grants, which have helped the district prepare for the next century and "made District 144 a model school district for technology," said Bill Browne, District 144 board of education president.

"Ms. Giles has provided the positive morale for the district and educational boost that is needed for our children as we move the school district into the 21st Century," Browne said.

Hank Dannenberg, director of curriculum for Tinley Park School District 140, said the district is trying to achieve more of a sense of security, in addition to technological advances.

"We're taking a good hard look at safety and security," Dannenberg

but now we're seeing if they is anything we can do even better."

Technologically, the district will have its six elementary school libraries automated by September. The district's two junior high schools already are equipped.

Video distribution systems will be linked up to individual classrooms, he said. The hook up to a 27-inch television will allow students to view work being done on an individual computer, or watch movies from the media center.

Strides are being made in the gifted education program and mentoring programs for kindergarten

important.

The characteristics include:
■ The definitions of "school," "teacher" and "learner" are reshaped by the digital world.
■ All students have equal opportunity for an outstanding education, with adequate funding, no matter where they live.
■ Educators are driven by high expectations and clear, challenging standards that are widely understood by students, families and communities.
■ A project-based "curriculum for life" engages students in addressing real-world problems.

secure, stimulating and a joyous learning environment that contributes to a lifelong passion for learning and high student achievement.
■ Leadership is collaborative, and governance is focused on broad issues that affect student learning.
■ Students learn about other cultures, respect and honor diversity and see the world as an extended neighborhood.
■ Schools promote creativity and teamwork at all levels and teachers help students turn information into knowledge and knowl-

edge into wisdom.
■ Assessment of student progress is more performance based, taking into account student individual talents, abilities and aspirations.
■ A student-centered, collaboratively developed vision provides power and focus for education community wide.
■ Continuous improvement is driving force in every school and school system.
■ Schools are the crossroads and central convening points of the community.

> "The definitions of schools and students as learners are changing because of technology. In fact the digital world is creating the change."
>
> Elizabeth Reynolds, superintendent
> Park Forest-Chicago Heights School District 163

The largest project a new school, Millennium Elementary, a kindergarten through fifth grade educational institution, will be opening next school year at 179th Street and 84th Avenue.

With these changes in mind, the south suburbs should boast some of the finest schools in the land.

Here is a listing of the 16 characteristics of schools and school systems throughout the country.

Implementation of the characteristics will make school districts capable of preparing students for global knowledge and information age.

As distributed by the American Association of School Administrators, the characteristics are not in order of priority. All are

issues important to humanity and questions that matter.
■ Teachers and administrators are effectively prepared for the global knowledge/information age.
■ Students, schools, school systems and communities are connected around-the-clock with each other and with the world through information-rich interactive technology.
■ School systems conduct considerable and significant research in designing programs that will constantly improve student achievement.
■ Students learn to think, reason and make sound decisions and demonstrate values inherent to democracy.
■ School facilities provide a safe,

WANT TO BE A SUPERINTENDENT?

G

H

2002 **Top Stories**

5

New hires, old fires

By JOHN HUSTON
STAFF WRITER

The top ten stories in Maywood and Broadview from 2002 are filled with new beginnings and sad endings, new management and mismanagement.

New leaders in District 89

1 The biggest changes came at Maywood-Melrose Park School District 89 in June, when two new administrators were hired.

Elizabeth Reynolds was named superintendent and John Jacobsen was named business manager.

Both came from Park Forest School District 163, where District 89 School Board President Charles Flower worked until July.

Flowers denied playing a major role in their hiring, saying, "I know they can do the job. These individuals are more than qualified. We are making an investment in the quality of our leadership team."

But suspicions were again raised the following month when six more District 163 employees, mostly administrators, were lured to District 89.

Reynolds said the district had a tight deadline to turn itself around and she didn't have time to train unqualified people.

"I have recruited some key people," she said. "I need firefighters that are ready to put out fires now."

The Herald reported in August that the former District 163 employees had received considerable pay increases, some as much as $25,000, in order to come to District 89.

"There's an old saying, 'You get what you pay for'," Reynolds said.

She also said that the salaries would be augmented by grants the district was planning on receiving.

The new administrative team also put together a new program at District 89 aimed at raising student academic performance.

Eight of the district's 10 schools had been put on last year's Early Academic Warning List for having less than 50 percent of students meet or exceed state standards for two consecutive years.

A new reading program, Direct Instruction, and math program, Saxon Math, were brought in by Reynolds' administrative team.

"Our expectation is to have kids reading in kindergarten," Reynolds said. "We will not have kids making it to third and fourth grades not reading."

The district also plans to start a foreign language program starting in third grade, as well as an eighth-grade requirement to master algebra.

Changing chiefs

2 Maywood also saw the hiring of a new police chief and the institution of a new community-policing program, with the intention of tackling the village's high crime rate.

Former Police Chief Luis Morales was forced into early retirement in February, opening a position that was filled by James E. Collier, Jr., who had been a captain of watch commander in Chicago's 11th police District.

Collier helped create the Maywood Alternative Policing Strategy program. It was modeled after Chicago's CAPS community-policing program.

The program split the village into beats, designated certain officers to work specifically in one beat and called for resident participation in order to identify and solve problems on a block-by-block basis.

It also helped link the Police Department to other village departments.

"Some of the problems that people may call about may not be a police problem," Collier said. "Through the communi-

Superintendent Elizabeth H. Reynolds speaks to administrators and teachers about improving the District 89 school system during a three-day session this summer.

ty-policing model, we can reach out to other departments in the village."

But violent crime in Maywood continued through the year, with at least 10 murders and scores of shootings reported through the middle of December.

Test scores 'dismal'

3 Test scores in Maywood's two school districts continued to lag behind state standards.

At Proviso Township High School District 209, student scores on the Prairie State Achievement Examination were lower in 2002 than the previous year across the board.

"The test scores are dismal," said Board President Theresa Kelly.

Proviso East averaged a score of 23.2 percent, compared to 28.1 in 2001.

Attendance, Kelly said, is the key to increasing student achievement.

Through a new procedure implemented this year, attendance was up by 15 percent over last year, Kelly said. Students who are chronically truant are sent to mandatory evening or summer school to separate them from other students.

In Elementary School District 89, six of the eight schools that were on the Early Academic Warning List made improvements on their test scores.

But four of the district's 10 schools still have fewer than 30 percent of students who met or exceeded the state's standards.

A new math and reading program implemented in Dis-

trict 89 will begin to show results in the coming years, officials said.

Funeral home closes

4 In a shocking display of mismanagement, the Drexel Funeral Home, 201 N. Second Ave., was the focus of an investigation by the State's Attorney's and Attorney General's offices.

The investigation was made public after a family arrived at the funeral home in August for the funeral of their newborn baby.

Family members found the home closed and the lights off inside.

When police arrived, the unembalmed body of the baby, was found in Drexel's basement in a partially opened

(Continued on page 6)

Hire Tough

> "Let us therefore come boldly unto the throne
>
> of grace, that we may obtain mercy,
>
> and find grace to help in time of need."
>
> (Hebrews 4:16 KJV)

H

One of the most critical tasks facing Superintendents is the building up of a competent staff committed passionately to students. When a district has an opening for a Superintendent position, there are many people who will apply. Certain individuals might have the appropriate licensure and academic training, but not really be passionate about developing the kind of children that need to be educated. What the person may be more concerned about is getting the check. It is extremely difficult to find good Superintendents who are truly committed to the cause.

In our many years of experience, the most effective Superintendents we have known came to the table not only with appropriate training and licensure but with the passion of a parent working to develop his or her own children. He or she took responsibility for all students in the district at all grade levels, all races, genders, and ethnic backgrounds. The conversation was always about doing what he/she needed to do to become better at delivering what the child needed.

These Superintendents we have known were constantly learning. They were interested in talking to other colleagues, taking every opportunity to continue growing. These conversations involved discussions about teachers who could be intentionally engaged in conversations about the children they were teaching as well as the students who were struggling or had ACES (Adverse Childhood Experiences.) However, these Superintendents were always positive, and we were confident they would prevail in the school district.

Scenario:

The principal, at some point, may become a Superintendent, although the Superintendent makes the initial recommendation to the Board of Education to hire the principal. It is, therefore, critical that many of the same attributes advertised for the Superintendent are also used to develop and refine the principalship.

The Superintendent has a strong responsibility to hire tough. Knowing what an excellent administrator looks like is key. The Superintendent sees either the quality the person has or the potential the person has. Hiring tough is important because an ineffective principal can cause many children to lose years of learning in school. There is no right for a child to have to fall into a never-ending cycle of failure. This is a dangerous trap. Every child has the right to have excellent teachers in an excellent school. Many students have failed, not because of their lack of knowledge but because the school was never able to offer what was needed. The school failed the child.

In David Cottrell's book Monday Morning Leadership (2009, p. 60), he shares that as leaders, we must hire tough, remembering that "1) The most important asset in your company is having the right people on your team. 2) Never lower your standards just to fill a position. You will pay for it later." He also shares two quotes from his mentor Tony Pearce (p. 97): "When it comes to leading people, there is no problem that is unique to you." "A real leader spends his time fixing the problem instead of finding who to blame."

If, by chance, you have an employee who needs to be terminated and it does have to happen, you must remember to dismiss the person with dignity. There is really no easy way to do this. I have shared with my cabinet members many times that I have never fired anyone—the person really fired themselves.

You will eventually have the task of dismissing an employee. This is part of the job. Firing, however, does not have to be difficult. The problem is that most individuals who are doing an unsatisfactory job already know they are in trouble. They are just waiting until you have the guts to tell them. Some administrators think that terminating an employee has to be tough for them, with late-night thoughts and sleepless nights. Not the case. I have always believed in documenting. When you come in as a new Superintendent, many times, your whole leadership team may need to be replaced. This may or may not come all at once; it depends on the severity of the problem. I shared that it is important to document everything, listen, and take your good mental notes. After collecting all of your data and listening to all of your key people, decisions will need to be made, and positions will need to be filled with the "right" people.

When you document, you have the hard evidence needed to "clean house" if necessary. This sounds cold. However, if you know in your heart that the person or persons are not contributing to the organization's work but are detrimental to the climate and culture of the team, then you must bite the bullet and do what you need to do: go through the steps (legal steps) needed to remove the person.

Hiring tough is also important because when you hire a leader, principal, or director to manage and lead a program in your school district, you are looking for results for the students. As Superintendent, sometimes I have recommended to the Board of Education the hiring of an administrator, and after several negative evaluations of the person, including providing mentoring and professional development, the team and I determine that the hire was not a fit because the person was not able to manage the program and get results. In addition, the person has alienated most of the staff, and everyone is just watching and waiting to see what you are going to do.

When an administrator is hired and is not working well in our district, and I determine (after much consideration and observation) that the person is not a fit, I begin the termination process. This is one of the most difficult decisions for me. However, the termination has to be done. The longer you wait, the worse it gets. Termination can also take a huge amount of time and energy. Not good! Since the task has to be done, you may as well do it. You must be clear about the evaluations, both formative and summative, and make a recommendation to the Board of Education to terminate, not renew, reassign to another slot, demote, etc. Termination is just as important as hiring. Make sure that you have documented, documented, and documented.

Hire people who:
1. Have the level of competence needed
2. Do not compromise your values and the values of the team
3. Can do more than one position if needed
4. Can measure up to your expectations
5. Can tell you the truth even if it hurts you

I have fired people, or people have fired themselves, because they:
1. Are insubordinate
2. Are slackers
3. Are liars
4. Misused funds
5. Hit a student
6. Have weak management skills
7. Are covering up for ineffective staff
8. Are providing tenure to ineffective teachers

Finally, hire tough, and by all means, *do not do the dance of the lemons.*

The dance of the lemons is real. This means that a leader knows that the teacher or person is ineffective yet does the despicable: passes on the individual to another person in order that the person continue to have a job, not considering the rights of the students. This is especially true in schools that have populations of predominantly black students. These are the students that seem to get "the short end of the stick," so to speak. The masses of black parents depend upon a strong public school to educate their children. Many of the parents may be low income, and because of their own lack of knowledge and positive experiences in school, they may not provide the extra support needed for their child. This means that these schools must have strong teachers who have a strong reputation for working well with predominantly black students in order to provide the extra support necessary for these black students to excel.

Many of us, as educators, have largely failed to recognize the crucial importance of culture in the lives of black children. Many of our children are in need of a trauma-sensitive environment, especially our black students. Research shows that in many predominantly black schools, the hiring of great teachers is not a priority. The hiring is sometimes last minute, which leads to hiring many leftover people. This can happen in many organizations, but it should not occur in school districts. This is not to say that hiring teachers at the last minute never results in attracting a great teacher, but most of the time, it does not. When we are concerned about students achieving at high levels, we want to be aggressive in early recruitment efforts. We should recruit, maintain, support, train, and retrain teachers in an attempt to make them into master teachers, with the goal being to grow the best and the brightest teachers for the school district, especially in predominantly black school districts.

H

I

INSPIRE

"All the effort in the world won't matter if you're not INSPIRED."

—Chuck Palahniuk

Inspire

> *"All Scripture is given by inspiration of God, and is profitable for doctrine, for reproof, for correction, for instruction in righteousness."*
> *(2 Timothy 3:16 NKJV)*

It is critical that we, as leaders, have the wherewithal to inspire other individuals to want to follow us. To inspire someone means to fill someone with the urge or ability to do or feel something, especially to do something creative. Synonyms include stimulate, motivate, encourage influence, move, stir, energize, galvanize, or incite.

It feels great as a leader when you work with someone, and you make that person feel that he or she wants to do anything you ask and knows they can do it because they are inspired. "Inspire" can also be defined as "to fill with an animating action or influence."

Good leaders do all of this. As Superintendents, we need to inspire our Board of Education and subordinates, as well as our community and any other group that has the opportunity to hear us speak. Serving as Superintendent, I (Elizabeth) have every opportunity possible to inspire different groups of individuals.

Kicking off the school year, I always make it a point to speak to these groups:

1. I hold a leadership team retreat for two or three days.

2. I speak at the first Board of Education meeting in August.

The purpose of this meeting is to set the tone for the year, review my mission and vision for the district, establish the Board of Education/Superintendent Goals, and share any new initiatives over the coming school year.

3.   I have a meeting with new teachers to set the tone, talk about the district's expectations, and share my vision of excellence for each school year.

4.   The district-wide meeting is organized and is held as a back-to-school parent orientation meeting. The parents understand that this meeting is to prepare them and their children for the new school year. I share:

- Student expectations
- School operating procedures
- Learning activities and parent involvement expectations for the school year

5.   The next inspirational meeting is held during the first week, back to school for all teachers. I speak at the Teachers Institute Meeting or first PD (Professional Development) meeting. This is a speech designed to inspire all staff, and to share the vision, the Board of Education Superintendent Goals and indicators, the district logo, and any past accomplishments and future initiatives.

6.   During the first week of school, I also invite all substitute teachers to a meeting to share expectations for substitute teachers in a session titled "How we do business in our school district." The meeting concludes with providing the individuals with a substitute teacher handbook. Many of the guest teachers are surprised that we thought enough of them to invite them to the district to a special meeting to visit with us.

7.   I will host a meeting with the leaders of the teachers' union and the union members. The purpose is to set the tone for each year and share common expectations.

8. I will meet with the local Chamber of Commerce. The purpose is to provide an update on the school initiatives, building plans, and events and expectations for each year, including new initiatives.

9. When we began our positions as new Superintendents in each school district that we served, we made a point of meeting with local churches in the surrounding community. We rotated from one church to the next until we felt comfortable that we had made an impact on the congregation. No matter what program the minister had for that Sunday, the minister always asked the Superintendent to say a few words.

    I spoke at Women's Day at one of the Baptist churches in one community. The purpose was to enlist the active aid and support of the churchgoing people in the education and development of our children and to reach out to business and professional community that they may know what we were trying to do and how they could support the children we served. Many of these people were big taxpayers—they can be of immense help and support to us.

10. I meet with a group of Superintendents (Joint Cooperative) in a common meeting place each month over the school year to discuss local, state, and national level updates in education.

11. In the community, we were involved each year in attending and participating in activities and programs like cancer walks, community parades, fine arts programs, plays, graduations, and many more. We provided great help and support in any program that we felt we were needed or called on to support.

The purpose is to be seen as being visible, active, and supportive. A Superintendent is a teacher in the same sense as a classroom teacher, except that the Superintendent's job is inspiring great teachers to become administrators.

Harry's favorite mentor was Marcus Foster, who said to Harry and his colleagues that one of his main tasks was to identify effective teacher leaders and to inspire, encourage, and motivate them to become Superintendents.

"A true leader has the confidence to stand alone,

the courage to make tough decisions, and the

compassion to listen to the needs of others. He does

not set out to be a leader, but becomes one by the

equality of his actions and the integrity of his intent."

- Douglas McArthur

INSPIRATIONAL LETTERS RECEIVED:

June 22, 1999

Dr. Elizabeth Reynolds

████████████████
████████████████

RECEIVED
JUN 24 1999
10:30

Dear Dr. Reynolds:

I want to reiterate in writing what I told you in person. "I do thank God that you came to School District ████" From the very start, I loved it when you said "children can be expected to learn". AMEN! As Janet pointed out at the last advisory committee meeting, we are beginning to hear a different response from parents in the community. They have had two years now to see the district is focused on a forward direction. Among numerous other things, I thank you and the Board of Education for working together to add Spanish to the curriculum. Now our students will have the jump on their future which will probably require them to be bilingual or multi-lingual

Because of this feeling of new life that is emanating from the school district, I am delighted that my granddaughter, ████████████████, who is a product of District ████ and ████ schools, had the opportunity to submit an application for teacher aide to the district. As you suggested when I asked you about it, she promptly applied when the ad appeared in the paper about ten days to two weeks ago. She realizes she received an excellent foundation in elementary education. It makes a parent and grandparent and resident proud to see that you have re-focused the educational goals that were apparent in the district's earlier years. RIGHT ON, DR. REYNOLDS.

I also noticed something my granddaughter wrote in her letter of application that I personally had forgotten about for a while. That is the fact that ████████ mentioned, in addition to helping the children learn, she wanted to have an opportunity to learn from them by experiencing and observing what kind of material holds their attention. She wants to learn from the children things that could help her in the future as she writes and illustrates children's books. Her statement brought back memories of what one of my children's teachers at Algonquin School in the mid-1960s remarked about what the children learn from each other and what the teacher can learn from the children and their interaction with others. COOL! I like that mutual learning process idea re-surfacing again.

Again, thank you, Dr. Reynolds. The cinnamon crispas are a Mexican type of cookie and I had mentioned to ████ that I wanted to say thank you also to the Board of Education for working so closely with you and introducing Spanish that maybe I would take the crispas to the Board meeting with a thank you note. ████ said they would probably like that but I thought, if you like the idea, I can always make more for the Board. I would like you to share this with your great office staff in the district. Just a small note of appreciation for their constant polite, helpful attitude. You can let me know what you think and I can always make more for the board. They're easy.

Barbara ████████████████

Dr. Reynolds

██████████████████████

Dear Dr. Reynolds:

I am writing this letter to you to express just how impressed I am with your school district's curriculum! We were fortunate enough during this past school year to have our daughter, █████ avail herself of all the amenities your district had to offer. She will enter the third grade this fall better prepared than most of her "private school" counterparts. We owe that to the "outside of the box" thinking and visionary leadership you have exercised in moving the school district forward. You have challenged our children (and their parents) to realize their full potential.

Whether it is the diversity encompassed in an art class on the works of Monet and Van Gogh, or the evolution of hermit crabs, the benefits reaped from your programs have had a positive impact on your students' growth. I have often thought of this school district as the "hidden treasure" or "diamond in the rough" of academic excellence in the south suburbs. Often times, people tend to identify the archdiocese or expensive private schools with "quality education." I firmly believe that if more people were cognizant of your district's capacity to bring a child's academic potential to fruition, that perception would change dramatically.

I would also like to commend you on the dedication and commitment to excellence exhibited by the staff you have assembled to lead your schools, specifically Principal ███████████████████████████ Their ingenuity and high work ethics truly make them a credit to their profession.

I look forward to immersing my daughter █████ in to this arena during the upcoming year. The seed of curiosity planted in █████ has found it's way to her younger sister, and what better environment to nurture it in than one that has yielded such positive results?

For everything you have done, and continue to do for "our" children, I thank you, and I look forward to speaking with you soon.

If you would like to contact me, I can be reached at ████████████ .

Sincerely,

Cynthia █████ (Parent)

MARGARET E. McDANNEL

MARGARET McDANNEL

September 20, 1999

School District #163 was in serious trouble. We had four superintendents in as many years. Senior school board members were resigning and the community was fed up with the entire system. New school board members were elected and even though they were inexperienced, they were dedicated to raising the scores and guaranteeing an education to all students. Therefore, this new board started from scratch. We hired an interim superintendent and spent a year in search of just the right superintendent. Someone who had the strengths necessary to make changes and turn this district around. We ended this search when we found Dr. Elizabeth Gaines Reynolds. Follow me as I take you down the road traveled by Dr. Reynolds in her quest for success and change for Park Forest/Chicago Heights School District #163.

When Dr. Reynolds took over at the helm, our Jr. Hi was in a dismal condition. Attendance was poor and the lack of discipline had the community up in arms. Parents were withdrawing their children from our schools and placing them in private schools. Moral among the teachers was extremely low. Our teachers had worked hard keeping the district together, but without adequate leadership or curriculum we were floundering. The Park Forest community knew what good education was. Our district had been a leader in education for years. We were always on the cutting edge for new programs. However, poor leadership and lack of updated curriculum in the last few years sent us spiraling into deterioration.

Dr. Reynolds first major act was a "Community walk". She held a breakfast on a beautiful Saturday morning in August and invited community leaders, teachers, administrators, board and parents to join her as she walked from school to school stopping in the community to talk to parents. We were like the Pied Piper of Hamlin following this beautiful woman. This was her way of getting to meet and know the community she was expected to lead. Dr. Reynolds offered her services as guest speaker to all civic organizations and churches to acquaint the community with her educational ideas for Park Forest. The community liked what they heard, however, they wanted more than words, they wanted action. They wanted to be able to walk down the halls of the Jr. Hi without taking their life in their hands. Discipline was definitely high on the community's wish list, as well as the strengthening the curriculum.

Where do you start to make change when attendance is low, tardiness is high, our scores are dropping each year, discipline is non-existent, the board was expelling students in groups and daily detention at the Jr. Hi was in the hundreds? Our most senior board member was ashamed to acknowledge that he was on the board at all.

Dr. Reynolds started by setting Goals for the District and set about immediately achieving those goals. The Jr. Hi administration was revamped. The position of Dean of Students was eliminated, a new principal was hired along with three assistant principals. One for each grade level. She supported this new administration with strong discipline policies. The moral among the teachers at the Jr. Hi saw a tremendous change immediately. Working as a team, the teachers and administrators have turned this school around. Dr. Reynolds also changed from a Jr. Hi. to a Middle School concept. It is a pleasure to walk down the halls now, even during passing time. An environment has been created whereby teachers can teach and children can learn.

Curriculum development was uppermost on Dr. Reynolds agenda. Each teacher was asked to make our a curriculum map showing what was taught and when. These maps were then placed end for end in grade order around the board room walls. It certainly did not take a rocket scientist to see the gaps, overlaps and unnecessary reviews. Dr. Reynolds demanded high expectations from all students, therefore a committee of teachers and administrators worked on creating higher standards with rigor and completing and upgrading the curriculum maps in all content areas.

To accomplish "Raising the Mark", Dr. Reynolds did several things simultaneously. She added eleven all day kindergarten with aides for each teacher, added Direct Instruction to the curriculum and Spanish as a language at the kindergarten level. The first year of all day kindergarten and Direct Instruction, our students were reading at first and second grade level as well as speaking Spanish. Direct Instruction did raise our scores after one year and we are now into our second year.

To help build vocabulary and spelling, Dr. Reynolds initiated the Superintendent's Word For The Day. A new word, with spelling, meaning and used in a sentence is given to every class from kindergarten through eighth grade each day. An award is given at the end of the year for those students who have mastered the Superintendent's Word for the Day.

During the summer, seminars are given for the teachers. Teachers teaching teachers, plus special consultants which Dr. Reynolds has hired. This program has been well attended and applauded by the teachers. This year Dr. Reynolds has added a once a month meeting for new teachers as a mentoring program. She also has a once a month meeting with a community advisory group, which helps her to keep her pulse on the needs of the community.

Our attendance has increased from 92% when Dr. Reynolds came to 98% last year and our enrollment has also increased tremendously. Dr. Reynolds is a hands on leader. She is in the schools every day, so she knows first hand what is going on and what needs to be changed. She has fought hard for the changes necessary to make this district a leader in education again. The Board has faith that Dr. Reynolds will again take the district to the cutting edge of education. She has made outstanding gains in accomplishing this in less than two years at the helm.

As a summary, Dr. Reynolds has accomplished the following:

1. Made the necessary changes in administrators
2. Added eleven all day kindergarten classes
3. Initiate Direct Instruction and Saxon Math
4. Strengthened our standards adding rigor
5. Added Spanish as a "grow program" at Kindergarten level
6. Superintendent's Word For The Day
7. Added a new 21st Century school containing 2 Kindergarten classes, Pre-K at risk Early Childhood, Birth to Three and Family Literacy.
8. Made presentations at State IASB Conferences
9. Serves on State Committee for Standards
10. Has four teachers also serving on state committees.
11. Increases reading scores
12. Increased enrollment
13. Increased attendance
14. Initiated inservice training for secretaries.
15. Revised, added and strengthened Policy Manual.
16. Changed Jr. Hi. to Middle School concept.
17. Held Board retreats and inservice training

This Board expected Dr. Reynolds to make bold changes. She has accomplished all of this in spite of having two new Business Managers in two years and a new staff in the District Office. Dr. Reynolds is to be admired for her courage to come to a new district as a first time Superintendent and make the changes she has. We commend her.

Respectfully submitted

Margaret McDannel

Margaret McDannel
Board President
School District #163

SCHOOL DISTRICT

89

COOK COUNTY, IL

BOARD OF EDUCATION SCHOOL DISTRICT 89

906 Walton, Melrose Park, Illinois 60160
Phone 708-450-2460

Grady Rivers, Jr.,
President

G. Ric Cervone,
Vice-President

Lequita Neely,
Secretary

Members:

Lisa Marea Anderson

Mary Lus Mendoza-Taylor

Joseph Parker

Marie Urso

April 24, 2004

To Whom It May Concern:

It is my pleasure to offer a letter of reference for Dr. Elizabeth H. Reynolds, former Superintendent of District 89, Maywood, Melrose Park, and Broadview. Dr. Reynolds joined our district in July 2002. I am a current board member of District 89 and a member of the board that selected Dr. Reynolds as our superintendent. Dr. Reynolds is and has been a professional in every sense of the word, always remaining focused on our district's goals and academic achievement.

Prior to joining our district our community was disconnected, uninformed and clueless about our educational status, our programs and what we needed. From the beginning Dr. Reynolds knew that in order to change the district and the community's mentality we would need to change the way our district conducted itself. Which meant that we needed to create an educational environment that informed all stakeholders of the state of our district and its academic status. She created avenues to communicate the information and recognized her staff's hard work in doing so.

There were many things that Dr. Reynolds did for our district that supported the changes she was implementing while maintaining focus and direction:

- Managed 10 schools, 12 buildings overall, over 400 teachers and staff members, and 6000 students
- Provided the Board with information and data of where our students were academically and arranged several planning meetings and community meetings to communicate those results and gave periodic updates
- Communicated the immediacy of complying with the NCLB requirements and implemented the Direct Instruction Reading Program and Saxon Math Program
- Required all schools to coordinate committees to create and implement their School Improvement Plans and emphasized the need to utilize it as a living and breathing document
- Utilized a consulting company to support teachers by modeling and training teachers to implement the reading program
- Instituted curriculum mapping to connect and align all programs and services
- Revamped the mentoring program for new teachers
- Reviewed, revised and implemented district policies and procedures
- Implemented teacher and staff development trainings on a monthly basis

- Hired a staff of professionals that assessed the district's current status and focused on our Special Education department to comply with state standards
- Worked with the Illinois State Board of Education departments to communicate our needs, comply with ISBE regulations and guidelines
- Arranged and facilitated many community events and committees: "District Wide Parent Meetings", "Superintendent's Advisory Committee", "New Teacher Network", "Student Leadership Academy", "Educational Leadership Academy", and the "Administrative Cabinet Meetings"
- Conducted board retreats and provided the board members with manuals and weekly, monthly and quarterly updates of district, state and local information
- Always met with parents and community members to provide open communication and provide an immediate response to their concerns
- Participated in several community committees and boards to maintain communication and coordinate efforts
- Held community events such as "Put Your Heart In To Education" to open the school's doors to all stakeholders
- Sought after several types of grants to supplement our financial needs, bringing over $2 million dollars to our district (never sought before)
- Believed in parental involvement, parent organizations and their daily participation in the schools
- Supported efforts to reach out to the Hispanic Community and arranged to have translators at our community, parent, and board meetings so that everyone received important district information
- Initiated a district wide breakfast program through our food services vendor for all students at no cost
- Recognized improvements along the way made by her staff and board members alike. She instituted a traveling plaque to recognize building improvements, student attendance, academic achievement and reaching professional development milestones

There were specific and calculated steps that Dr. Reynolds took to achieve the district goals. She was tireless in her attempt to coordinate groups of people to get involved in such a short period of time and she left no stone unturned. She embraced diversity and took the negative factors as a challenge to change it and turn it towards a positive and productive path. Her words "Stay Focused" were repeated over and over to us in the efforts that it would become second nature and it is. Dr. Reynolds is very passionate about the right to educate all children. It permeates through her and she glows when she witnesses real education-taking place through effective instruction.

Dr. Reynolds' background, experience, training, and skills are impressive. She is an accomplished person who has clearly dedicated her life's work to her academic career. The confidence and belief that all children can learn is motivating and contagious and Dr. Reynolds believes that, with all that she is. As a parent who has children in our district it was crucial to me to bring in someone into our district who was clearly focused on getting our students back on track. Dr. Reynolds utilized her team to identify methodically where the students were currently and placed them on a plan to bring them to grade level and above. She didn't shy away from the tough questions or telling the hard truths about what our district was facing. Her dedication to utilizing data to guide her and the Board in educational decisions was first and foremost to her. She often asked the question "How will this move kids?" which she asked before and after a decision was finalized.

Dr. Reynolds is greatly missed not only by me, but also by parents and community residents. She has created a standard that will be hard to change and tough to match. Her caliber of people has never been present within a leadership position in our district or our community before and her absence has created a great void.

Dr. Reynolds believes in accountability, high expectations, raising the bar, training, professional and personal development and a quality education for all and thanks to her we believe now that we not only require it, but we deserve it. She will be an asset to any school district; educational institution or organization and I wish her all the success.

Sincerely,

Mary Lus Mendoza-Taylor
School Board Member
District 89, Maywood, Melrose Park and Broadview

PROVISO TOWNSHIP HIGH SCHOOLS
District No. 209 - Cook County

GREGORY T. JACKSON
SUPERINTENDENT

807 South First Avenue
Maywood, Illinois 60153

Telephone: (708) 344-7000
FAX: (708) 344-1228

October 2003

To Whom It May Concern:

I am pleased to write a letter of recommendation for Dr. Elizabeth H. Reynolds. I have worked with Dr. Reynolds directly over the last two (2) years as she has been serving as Superintendent of School District 89, one of my elementary feeder districts.

I had previous knowledge of her work prior to assuming the role as Superintendent in the Maywood-Melrose Park-Broadview communities. Her reputation as a leader in the field of education is well known. She has been described as an outstanding, results-oriented, instructional leader.

While she has served in such a key leadership role, she has gained respect from all of her constituents. Administrators, support staff, and parents respect her because she has actually been in schools and on the playgrounds talking to and working with them. She has organized and taught staff development sessions for certificated and non-certificated staff.

As a researcher and practitioner, she has continued to share the data with the community and has kept the community up to date on best practices in the field.

In November 2003, Dr. Reynolds and I will be co-presenting two proposals at the IASB/IASA/IASBO Joint Conference in Chicago. The titles of the presentations are **"Creating Effective Schools – Empowering Broad Based Support"** and **"Systemic Reform – Establishing a Sense of Urgency."** This is an honor for both of us; however, Dr. Reynolds has routinely made presentations all over the country. She has presented at the National School Board Association (NSBA), American Association of School Administrators (AASA), and the IASB/IASA/IASBO Joint Conference each year.

I appreciate the work that Dr. Reynolds is doing with improving achievement of her students in District 89. I congratulate her for the achievement gains (Terra Nova and ISAT) made in one (1) year for the 2002-03 school year. I am grateful because her students will come to my high school district more fully prepared.

Dr. Reynolds' commitment to all children has paid off for the total District 89 and 209 communities!

Sincerely,

Gregory T. Jackson
Superintendent

134

September 3, 1999

When Elizabeth Reynolds came to Park Forest-Chicago Heights, District 163, test scores were declining each year. There were serious concerns about the reading scores (this was true for the whole State of Illinois). We did not have a specific curriculum. We had the State Goals and outcomes, but the vehicle (curriculum) to achieve those goals was not in place. There were huge gaps and repetitions. Additionally, there was frequent turnover in superintendents, and parents were putting their children in private schools. **This is what Elizabeth walked into!**

Elizabeth met with the Union leadership. The Union leaders expressed concern about the lack of a specific curriculum, the lack of effective staff training and the lack of good discipline policies which addressed behavior, absences, and tardiness. There was a desire to improve the district.

Elizabeth made it clear to staff that she was here to improve student achievement! By the first day of school, plans were in place for curriculum mapping. We started with math. ALL staff was involved at building meetings. Grade level groups met and outlined everything each person taught in math the previous year (a "no-fault list"). These lists were transferred to a monthly chart. All charts were posted (from pre-K to 8th grade). Gaps and repetitions were addressed. Teachers requested training they needed. Classes were held. The maps were posted outside each classroom and we were on our way! Teachers and para-professionals found out that one of the greatest benefits of mapping was the dialogue it opened among staff— ideas, materials and strategies were shared. (Because of this focus and clear delineation of what was to be taught, test scores improved the first year of the mapping.)

What else did Elizabeth Reynolds do to make parents and staff want **their** children in our schools? All kindergartens became full day programs. Spanish instruction started in kindergarten. She held community forums and asked members of both communities what they expected from our schools. At each Board meeting, students read their own stories or poetry, explained projects that they had done in class, played musical instruments—all examples of excellence! Showcasing students' achievements at Board of Education meetings attracted many parents, grandparents, and friends to the meetings. As a result, there was more positive community involvement in education. The School Board developed and approved policies for attendance, tardiness and discipline. Student handbooks and employee handbooks clearly outlined rules, procedures and expectations.

At the beginning of Elizabeth's second year, she worked with the Union to plan five days of teacher training in Direct Instruction prior to the opening of school. The entire staff (teachers and paraprofessionals) was trained in the Reading Mastery Program. During the first week of school, all children in the district were tested, reading groups were formed and by the second week of school, Direct Instruction in reading was in place. All kindergartners were in the Reading Mastery I program. Parents were amazed that by Christmas, their kindergarten children were blending sounds and sounding out words. There was enthusiasm about the reading progress by the students. Parents who initially objected to the program came to Board meetings to express their enthusiasm, and the pride they felt that their child was reading. Parents started feeling more positive about school. Test scores in reading, math and language arts improved. Discipline is better because students are "on task".

Outstanding student achievement must be the mission for all school districts regardless of race, gender, socio-economic status or the personal circumstances of the student! The teachers and the para-professionals must have the "tools" and the training to most effectively use these tools. Elizabeth Reynolds provided these tools and she provided the leadership in effecting great changes **for the students in District 163!** Her commitment to student achievement and staff training has made a difference!

Sincerely,

Barbara Ruggles, Retired Teacher and Past President, Teachers' Federation of Park Forest A Council of A.F.T. Local 604

J

JOY

Joy

> "Behold, this is the joy of his way,
>
> and out of the earth shall others grow."
>
> (Job 8:19 KJV)

As Superintendent, you are communicating with several distinct groups: students, parents, teachers, administrators, and the board. An effective way to do this is to exhibit a disposition of joy and warmth as supposed to a stony face that says, "I am not approachable." Joy comes about when you use good judgment, since you are always making a decision about something. These decisions can be life-changing for children and staff. Therefore, the person making the decisions needs to exercise a great deal of wisdom and warmth.

A Superintendent has to use good judgment, as he/she will be evaluated by the Board of Education at least once a year. The evaluation will reflect the Superintendent's judgment in several areas. One of those areas involves your demeanor (how you relate to others). A Superintendent feels good or joyful when the evaluation rating is good. On the other hand, please do not get out of sorts because the board has some areas of improvement for you. Even if you do not agree, there is no room for being confrontational. It is always good to "take it on the chin." The basis of a high-quality Board/Superintendent relationship, and a productive Superintendent evaluation, is to look at areas that can be worked on or improved. Please do not be afraid of the evaluation. This is a time to pay attention and, if needed, be still and listen.

These are documents designed to detail the responsibilities of the Superintendent and express the expectations of the board (Illinois Association of School Boards, 2014):

1. Superintendent's contract

2. Position description

3. District's mission and vision and goals statements

4. School Board of Education policies

5. Strategic plan

6. Professional standards

J

November 25, 2019

Dear Elizabeth:

Thank you for your participation at the Joint Annual Conference in Chicago. The information, insight, and expertise you offered helped make this conference a tremendous event.

It takes the combined talents of many people such as yourself to make an educational conference a success. Know that your contribution was sincerely appreciated.

Thank you, again, and have a wonderful Holiday Season.

Sincerely,

Jenny Harkins
Administrative Assistant

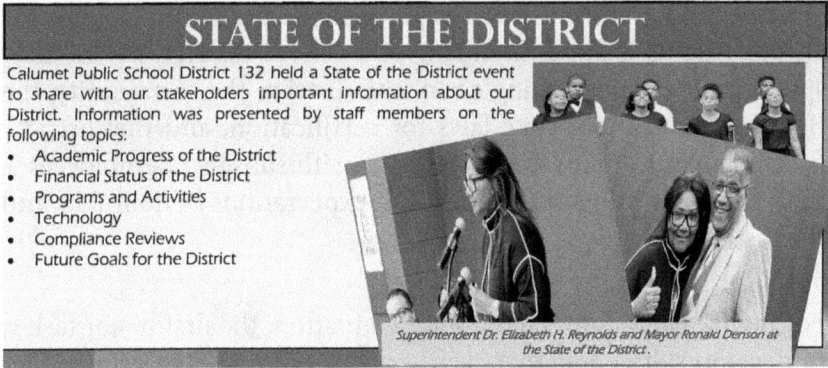

STATE OF THE DISTRICT

Calumet Public School District 132 held a State of the District event to share with our stakeholders important information about our District. Information was presented by staff members on the following topics:

- Academic Progress of the District
- Financial Status of the District
- Programs and Activities
- Technology
- Compliance Reviews
- Future Goals for the District

Superintendent Dr. Elizabeth H. Reynolds and Mayor Ronald Denson at the State of the District.

A sense of joy also comes about when you have worked with your board to finalize the Essential Board of Education Process Agreements. This makes life run more smoothly for you and the board.

These sample items were taken from an instrument used by an IASB Field Representative (December 2017):

- How often will the Board of Education and the Superintendent meet?

- How often will the Superintendent communicate with the board?

- How does the Superintendent respond to questions from the board?

- What One Knows, All Know—Whenever one board member asks a question, the question and the response are provided to all board members.

- The rule of NO SURPRISES from the Board of Education or Superintendent.

- Only two people are allowed to talk to the press: the Superintendent and the Board of Education President.

When a novice administrator is planning or preparing to apply for an opening as a Superintendent of a school district, he/she may spend much time learning about the district, the community, the Board of Education, state laws for certification, and the district's fiscal history, to name a few. An issue with subsets of employees is their understanding of the goals and expectations of their jobs and the district.

For novice candidates facing such a situation, the first major task is to develop statements that clearly define what the Superintendent proposes to do, who will be responsible for getting it done, and how progress toward that goal will be measured. There is a lot of joy in preparing for a new position as Superintendent.

EXAMPLE EMAIL

Superintendent Office:

Dr. Reynolds,

The CEA is looking forward to a new school year! We have a fresh start to the year with a new contract and revitalized union board. We are pleased with how well the administration and the union have worked together and wish to continue this relationship in the future.

With this in mind, we wanted to address the concerns of our members with you right away. A big concern is a staff member needing to take their children to college. College is a monumental achievement in the life of students, and we want to encourage all of our students to attend.

In the contract, we have the new clause that personal days may be used for parents to take their children to college.

We know that our staff needs to gain your approval when it occurs during Institute Days. We know the importance of attending the Institute Days to prepare ourselves for the school year. However, when a child is going away to school, especially their first time, it is difficult, almost impossible, for parents to make the decision between work and their families.

We know that in the past, these days have not been approved. We are asking that, in the future, they are approved. This gesture of goodwill can help create a positive culture in our district.

Thank you for your consideration

Harry: My elementary school principal never smiled, and he did not exhibit warmth. My perception of him and a few other teachers was fear. Many administrators and teachers felt that showing signs of warmth and happiness toward children would be interpreted by the children as a weakness. Nothing can be farther from the truth, in my judgment. The mantra in all schools, and especially in elementary school, is that the school should be a joyous and happy place. Working as Superintendent, we must become vulnerable. Vulnerability is contagious. "It spreads, like a smile or a compliment or a good deed. The more you voice your vulnerabilities, the more you empower yourself in any situation, and the more power and control you have" (Adam Harris, Illinois School Board Journal, March/April 2019).

Being able to accomplish and share with the community all of the great things and successes of your district will bring you so much joy and happiness. See the next page for a speech I shared with the community that brought everyone much joy!

143

OPENING SPEECH SAMPLE:
STATE OF THE DISTRICT REPORT

Good Evening and Welcome

As Superintendent, I think it is appropriate from time to time that we give a State of the District report to you our constituents (stakeholders). Several months ago, the leadership team and I made a presentation to the Board and community. From the feedback that we have received; the event was worthwhile and appreciated.

The session this evening is designed to inform you of progress made to date and remind you of:

1. My vision for the District

2. Academic Progress

3. Compliance Updates

4. Technology Update

5. Fiscal Status of District – Past, Present and Future

Some leadership team members will provide individuals updates that are specific to their department or area of expertise.

Our reports will highlight progress toward achieving the 7 Board/ Superintendent GOALS developed and approved in a regular Board meeting.

There's nothing that is Done in Isolation. Effective organizations are guided by written policies which define in detail what should be done, when it should be done and who is responsible for making certain it is done in an environment where all students feel safe physically, emotionally and academically. (How will you inspect what you expect).

My vision is that we continue to create a child-centered school district: with a clear and focused academic mission. A vision of all students Pre-K – 8th understanding the benefits of a college education and all the opportunities they would have.

1. A District known by staff members committed to high expectations for academics and behavior for all students and themselves.

2. A District governed by a strong student focused Board whose primary purpose is the development of our children and places children and the needs of children 1st.

3. Strong instructional leaders – where Principals work to create a positive work environment and is supportive of all teachers working hard to make a difference.

4. Sufficient learning time so students are fully prepared and frequent monitoring of students' progress to ensure students success as outlined in ESSA – Every Student Succeeds Act.

5. A clean and safe environment – look around the schools as with all of our buildings – working to install a sense of pride and ownership.

6. Climate of High Expectations and High Standards where we believe in our students and their success and our students help us to know what our students must know and be able to do at any point and time over the school year.

7. Finally, strong parental involvement in schools where parents are involved, academic achievement levels rise. Parents you are your child's 1st and most important teacher.

The focus of our work over the past years has involved a very COMPREHENSIVE REFORM approach. This is an approach where by a district aims to revitalize itself by improving ALL aspects of its operations, ...rather than implementing or seeking to improve isolated programs. This work cannot be done in a PIECEMEAL Fashion.

While areas of concern were clearly evident, School Improvement is a continuous process...and we are continuing our work to improve the teaching and learning of ALL students and staff in our district... on a daily basis.

You have heard the words Strategic Plan. As I think about our Strategic Plan in our District: Our plan is more than works in a book or on a wall. One researcher said, "If everything is important, then nothing is Important". That is the purpose of having only 7 agreed upon and approved Board Superintendent/Goals. The first Goal being to improve Curriculum and Instruction for All students.

Because of our Culture of Excellence and our committed staff, we have received many National and State Awards in our District. From our National P.R. Awards, Those Who Excel State Award, Financial Recognition Award every year, 100% Compliance Award yearly for Health/Life Safety, to our Golden Apple Foundation Leader Award for Outstanding Leadership, to name a few.

It is a great time to be a part of this District. Several years ago, this was not the case. Is the District perfect, no there is no perfect school district anywhere. Because we deal with real people, real lives and real students. We have real facts to share about our District and we are proud to report this evening, as a leader real proud of the Board.

The Board developed and approved 7 Board Superintendent Goals for the District. These 7 Goals and indicators drive our Strategic Plan and our Long and Short-Range Goals.

K

KNOWLEDGE

Knowledge

> *"Let the wise hear and increase in learning,*
>
> *and the one who understands obtain guidance."*
>
> *(Proverbs 1:5 ESV)*

Know what you are getting into before you agree to work as a Superintendent. It is important that you understand that this is a very complex job. The principal focus should be on the academic and social and emotional development of children.

K

As you find yourself moving toward leadership, think about what that means relative to your behavior and focus. A Superintendent needs to know the range of instruction for which he/she is accountable. In a relay race, for example, each runner is placed in his/her position because of demonstrated excellence in the speed required at that time. If you are an elementary school Superintendent, you are responsible for building the elementary foundation upon which all instruction is based. In many states, such as Illinois and California, the makeup of school districts ranges from unit districts (K-12), elementary districts (typically K-8), and high school districts (typically 9-12).

If you are selected to lead a district, you must become knowledgeable of the segment that you will lead and all of the requirements. If you have a high school district, you must know the required subjects for entrance into college as well as for graduation. You also need to know what kinds of scores your students need to enter various colleges: SAT, ACT, etc. You need a good understanding of what post-high school opportunities are available for your students. If a student is interested in vocational education, then you need to know what opportunities exist for students at the lowest cost. On the other hand, if you take on the position of an elementary school Superintendent, the curriculum still needs to introduce the children to the various ways people earn a living, starting with the obvious things around them—policeman, fireman, banker, engineer, doctor, lawyer, farmer (take them to a real farm). As they progress up through the grades, they are introduced to more sophisticated professions.

Once you have agreed to accept the position at whatever level, you should demonstrate a working knowledge and understanding of all of these important areas:

- Up-to-date strategic plan
- Long- and short-range goals
- School Board of Education policies
- Administrative procedures
- CBAs (Collective Bargaining Agreements)
- Financial checks and balances (last five audits)
- Elected officials in the community (to build a good working relationship)

Many of these concerns will come out of your regular one-to-one communication with the board members.

We believe that particularly in the first year of your tenure, you should meet on a consistent basis, one on one, with each board member. We found this to be extremely beneficial. This in no way precludes working closely with the board president on a regular basis, though some board presidents may not want you to have regular meetings with individual members. In order to avoid confusion and conflict, this is a procedure that must be worked out with all board members in a retreat where you have agreed upon

Board/Superintendent communication and procedures. It would not hurt to have a new Superintendent encourage the board to have short retreats on a quarterly basis.

- Know the board
- Know the community
- Know the staff
- Know the students
- Know the teachers
- Know the union
- Know the pitfalls
- Know the strengths

Research the issues that the community is facing. Talk to your peer Superintendent colleagues. Talk to other leaders in the community. Find out where the land mines are. Know about the politics of the district. Look at the past Board of Education agendas. Find any reviews or comments on social media. What is the funding like? Look at grants, including competitive grants. Is there a balanced budget? How long has it been balanced? How much is allocated for board spending? Is there a procedure for board spending, including Board of Education conference travel? Do you have policies that control spending for a staff, administrator, Board of Education? Look at the achievement data trend by grade level and teachers. Where are the gaps at each school? How has the district gotten along with the community? Research FOIA (Freedom of Information Act) requests. What are the hot-button topics being requested? What is the relationship with the teachers' union, administrative team, Board of Education, community, and teachers?

Know your strengths and know your shortcomings. Know yourself—know who you are. There is a saying that "if you can't take the heat, get out of the kitchen." As Superintendent, you will be criticized. It comes with the job, especially if you are trying to effect change and you are stepping on somebody's toes. Learn how to take criticism. Sometimes it will be painful; people may say mean things about you. If it is true, do what you need to do to change, and do not get mad about it. On the other hand, it's important to communicate and even over-communicate (you can always back off). Have critical friends you can talk to who will give you honest feedback, perhaps including a Superintendent colleague or friend.

LEGAL KNOWLEDGE

Starting with accepting the position as CEO or Superintendent, it is essential that you have a lawyer to work with you on your potential contract. You can be sure the Board of Education who is hiring you is working with their attorney on ideas for a suitable contract. Your ideas and the Board's ideas for a contract should be worked on simultaneously. It is critical that you have legal advice because you are beginning a relationship with a board (a marriage), and when I have worked with Superintendents during the time of divorce (leaving the district on not-so-good terms) legal language has always prevailed—whatever is in the contract prevails. If you slipped up on your contract, then you ruined an opportunity to leave on your terms. On another note, legal knowledge is important because in conducting the day-to-day business of the district, including legal business, you must have the discernment to know when to call the district lawyer and when not to. You must always remember:

1. The lawyer works for the board.

2. You are paying big bucks every time you make contact with the lawyer (every time you dial the phone).

3. Remind all staff to ask for permission to call the lawyer. This is done to keep the district running smoothly and to make sure not everyone is calling. Usually, all legal calls come through the Superintendent's office.

As you approach a new district as Superintendent, one of the ground rules or expectations of your staff is that no one makes a call out to the district attorney unless you, the Superintendent, have directed them. If there is no control over this issue (protocol), the district can "bleed out" or go broke—be in deficit spending. Lawyers will always rejoice when you call—remember, they are paid well at an hourly rate for handling simple problems. I am not undermining lawyers, because they can be a tremendous asset.

For example, when you are in the process of developing your contract, you need the advice of a knowledgeable lawyer to make certain it contains the exact items needed: length of time, number of years (multi-year or one-year), mileage, professional development days, etc.

If the board feels that you have done an excellent job in your first year as Superintendent, even if you have a one-year contract, it is more than likely that the board will want to keep you. At that time, you will need a lawyer to work on the extension of the contract. We have been blessed to always have the support of a majority of the board, and we have had multi-year contracts where the boards immediately extended our contracts before each one ran out. These multi-year contracts had the stipulation of being performance-based and tied to specific goals and indicators. Over our lifetime as Superintendents, some years have been extremely difficult.

Elizabeth's Reflections:

In my first year as Superintendent, I used the knowledge that I brought into the district to professionally develop large groups of people in the community. On one evening, I trained these individuals, teachers, administrators, board members, and community members, including politicians. I wanted to prepare them to lead groups of community patrons in answering questions and providing input in order to build our strategic plan. After I trained all of these individuals, they were prepared to give leadership in our large community forum. I never lost contact with these individuals, and they became some of my most knowledgeable and loyal supporters.

My third superintendency was in a district that needed an

experienced Superintendent to "turn the district around," which was absolutely the case. I was recruited to take the job because the district was broken. It was in such disarray that I knew the only way to go was up. Stakeholders had made negative statements about the district because it had a history of failure and had earned a negative reputation based on that track record. I have been in this district for over 13 years now, and I am proud of this district. It is a safe and beautiful place for children. The children are progressing academically, and the finances have been balanced for all 13 years.

Again, students are learning, and the district has been a great place for students to achieve because of academics, finances, new buildings, and beautiful grounds. We received Excellent 100% Health/Life Safety reviews over the years and excellence awards because of our decline in insurance rates due to a low number of accidents. We have shared our "journey to success" every year at our State Conference in Illinois, realizing that success is never final. It is all about continuous progress. The board and community, the mayor, and the chamber are all proud of the district now. Their support is phenomenal.

A major problem with many inexperienced Boards of Education is that the board does not have the capacity or knowledge to interpret contracts for Superintendents, principals, teachers, and support staff. Therefore, they are prone to make mistakes, which can result in the district having to spend huge legal fees and penalties to solve a contractual issue with an administrator, teacher, custodian, clerk, or principal.

As it relates to legal knowledge, you should become familiar with these areas: litigation (especially any litigation the district is currently involved in), collective bargaining (including arbitrations), mediations, student discipline (expulsions), special education, school finance matters, tax rate issues, bond issues, tax anticipation warrants and notes, tax objections, and real estate matters.

Some recent legal topics of discussion include the impact of Senate Bill 100 in the State of Illinois mandated in September of 2016, transgender student discrimination, concussion legislation, the Open Meeting Act, preparing for due process hearings for special education, fiscal crisis in your state, and pitfalls to avoid in dealing with teacher non-renewals.

Legal knowledge also includes becoming familiar with the state's Education Code, all board policies and administrative procedures, and Collective Bargaining Agreements (CBAs). Upon my arrival as Superintendent in two districts that I served, it became apparent to me that a major underlying cause of the fiscal deficit was huge monetary payouts to staff members who had sued the district. This travesty was caused because of a lack of legal knowledge. One principal was fired, and the board paid out over $50,000 to her because the district had not honored her contractual agreement. A teacher who was fired and sent home without pay sued the district and won, because the legal requirement was that the teacher should have been sent home with pay until the board approved the recommendation to withheld pay.

Another administrator had sued the district three or four times and was still working in the district—not that a person cannot sue a district and still work there, but this administrator successfully sued and won all three or four times. This was really different for me. One time, a person sued because she tripped and fell over some extension cords. The district had cords hanging all over offices and classrooms. The district had not passed any Health/Life Safety audits, and I could understand why. I knew what I needed to do.

In the district where I have served for over 15 years, there have been many occasions to terminate administrators, teachers, and support staff for cause. I knew legal knowledge was needed. Therefore, I worked with the attorney and followed all policies and procedures, and I always ended up winning our district cases. For over ten years prior to my accepting the position of Superintendent there, the district had been in chaos. The district was wastefully spending huge amounts of district funds on legal fees and penalties. Needless to say, in one year's time, the budget was balanced, and it has been balanced in every subsequent year and has received financial recognition for every single year of my superintendency. The district's reserves have grown from nothing ten years ago to over $20 million. This has occurred while totally remodeling two schools and building a brand new school without going out for a referendum.

Harry's Reflections:

K

Know your district and be known by your clientele, students, and support staff. Interact with everyone on a positive basis whenever possible. Make sure students and staff know you as a person and show that you care about them personally. Be visible in the community, especially in informal settings. Don't gain an image of being aloof and unapproachable, too busy for ordinary people and too busy to spend time interacting with children or support staff. Make sure to take time to visit and cultivate support staff. Don't become a prisoner of your appointments with "people who are important" while neglecting the organization's delivery of "deliverables" for children. Plan and reserve time to really visit schools and classes, not just blow in and out. Take or make time to talk and interact with people so they may get to know you. This is how you get in the trenches and attain firsthand knowledge. Fist bump your staff, including custodial staff and community workers.

Some time ago, shortly after I began serving as vice principal of a new urban high school, I asked the daughter of a friend who was a freshman in a suburban high school about her transition and adjustments to the new and larger environment. I asked if she knew the name of the principal, and if she had seen or met him personally. Her response was negative. I repeated this question over several months with the same response. I concluded there were no positive efforts made for students to know who the principal was by name or in person.

I resolved that should I become principal, I would make every effort to know my students by name, by beginning my journey in the new school with a welcome meeting and thereafter being available to eat lunch with my students in order to chat with them about whatever they wanted. Eating lunch with students frequently resulted in me "watching my lunch being eaten" while we talked—depending upon what was on the menu. In my early days as vice principal, this strategy helped me to know my student body by name and sight. I also knew the families of many because I attended church in the community. This also applies to the position of Superintendent. Go to schools to see classrooms, not just to be introduced, but to see what is going on. There will be opportunities for students to meet you.

THOUGHTS FROM A SUPERINTENDENT

When a candidate is considering applying for an opening, it is important to learn as much as possible about the district: its successes, problems, the kind of community, the community's perception of the quality of the schools, the standing as it relates to performance in all schools and the district. A candidate also needs to know how the schools stack up on national data. Look at all of the hard data you can get.

Visit the district and neighboring areas and sites such as libraries, and read the local news, which might give helpful insight into the district.

Harry's Reflections:

My first job as Superintendent was a blessing in so many ways. One of these was the school board, because they had no desire to "run" the district. They made it clear they hired me to manage the district and would work with me to achieve our common goal. Because we were working on common goals, our communication was open and honest, and there were no surprises during my tenure. With such a Board of Education, I was free to work on our jointly agreed-upon goals and objectives and any other issues that surfaced. One of my management practices was my regular visits to schools, classrooms, and maintenance shops. Our district office, maintenance shops, and high schools occupied almost a section of land. Although we had a fleet of buses, we had a small garage for repairs and maintenance. The district was blessed with a creative group of mechanical staff led by an insightful lead mechanic. Because the repair garage was near where I parked, I had many opportunities to see their projects.

In that period, most of the districts in our area all used the same brand of school buses, most of which were of the same vintage: when a district retired an old bus, we would purchase it and use it for repair parts. Our neighbors soon discovered we could repair their buses faster and at a lower cost and thereby not lay off our crew (due to Proposition 13). When the mechanic crew was "caught up" on regular work, they would rebuild engines, transmission, and other parts to facilitate quick turnaround of repairs. This meant we had key parts in storage ready to be installed. Our crew was able to run this operation with only two under-cover pits. Such clever technicians saved significant dollars and jobs during the long period of leveling up. Such behavior was possible because of the knowledge on the part of the Superintendent and Board of Education, both of which encouraged creative input. I loved it! Have knowledge!

Elizabeth's Reflections:

In 2020, serving as superintendent of any school district has been called challenging, to say the least. Many of our school communities have been negatively impacted during these unprecedented times by the COVID-19 pandemic. Supporting students and families through this pandemic is paramount for all of us: the Board of Education, Superintendent, principals, administrators, teachers, and support staff.

COVID-19 is imposing novel and unforeseen questions for everyone. A common experience for many school districts and families during this crisis is the loss of jobs and income. Our district quickly transitioned to remote learning options to prevent the spread of COVID-19, and we continue to support our students as we navigate these new challenges. We have distributed laptops to students and have provided free internet to parents who needed these resources. We introduced online events and conferences such as our first annual remote Parent/Teacher Conferences and our monthly Virtual Parents' Night Out event.

Thanks to the dedication of our staff and our diligence in securing multiple grants, we have been able to provide consistent breakfast, lunch, and dinners for our community through our Grab and Go program, which provides meals for all children 18 and under. Our district also initiated an e-learning program so that our students could continue to learn while school buildings are closed because of the pandemic. We additionally launched our "Academic Bus" program, which delivers work packets to our students throughout the district.

My goal as a leader and learner is to provide all necessary materials and supplies needed for my staff, students, and community. This forced me to step up to the plate and become an expert in virtual learning. I have attended virtual board meetings, professional development sessions, evaluations with administrators, and national, state, and local conferences.

The results of our online and phone call surveys confirmed that full remote learning was recommended by the majority of our parents and community. And, because of the COVID-19 positivity rate in our district, I recommended to my Board of Education that we move forward with full remote learning for all students, which allowed our students to continue their education in a safe environment. As of September 29, 2020, our instructional program continues to combine online lessons and self-paced activities to engage students and create personalized learning experiences to meet all of the needs of our students. Our students work in synchronous and asynchronous sessions with teachers and classmates via tools/ devices.

Video Conference with Teachers and Staff

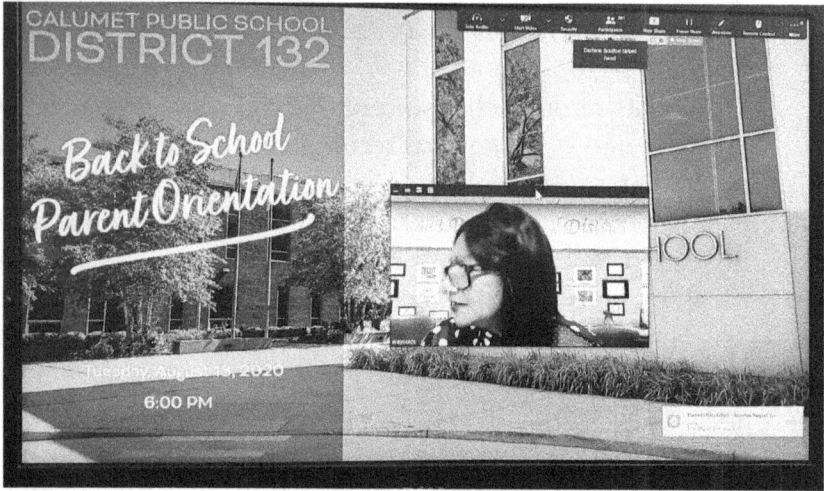

*Video Conference at Back to School Orientation
with Families and Staff*

K

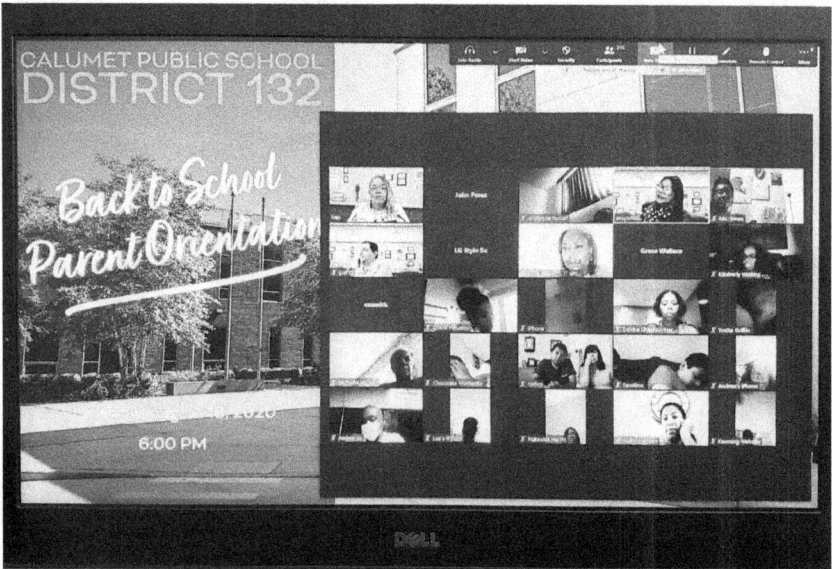

Video Conference with Cabinet Team

Video Conference with Cabinet Team

K

*Praying with Leadership Team Members
during Video Conference*

WANT TO BE A SUPERINTENDENT?

K

L

LISTEN

*"One of the best ways
to persuade others is with
your ears."*

—Dean Rusk

Listen

> *"My dear brothers and sisters, take note of this:*
> *Everyone should be quick to listen, slow to*
> *speak and slow to become angry."*
> *(James 1:19 NIV)*

Be honest, be consistent, be considerate, be courageous, and by all means, listen.

Leadership facilitator John Hester writes that "the ability to truly listen is one of the most important skills we can develop in this life." When he has asked workshop participants, "How many of you have had formal training in listening?" he has noticed that only about 10 percent raised their hands. Hester writes: "Listening is such a critical skill—and yet so few have been trained in it…. Dictionary. com defines the word listen as follows: 1. To give attention with the ear; attend closely for the purpose of hearing. 2. To pay attention; heed. Yes, it means to hear; but it also means to pay attention—with our ears, our eyes, and our hearts. True listeners look beyond the words themselves—they search for meaning in the speaker's tone and body language" (John Hester, "What Does It Mean to Really Listen?" LeaderChat, August 2013).

Hester continues: "Not only is listening to others a key life skill, it can also have a tremendous impact on building trust in a relationship. When we take the time to listen, we show the other person that we care—that we are interested in understanding their perspective. That can go a long way toward building, or rebuilding, a relationship." Life coach Caren Osten notes: "Research shows that only about 10 percent of us listen effectively. We are so distracted by the cacophony of dings and tweets from our smartphones, not to mention our ever-growing to-do lists, that we struggle to focus and listen when people talk to us" (Caren Osten, "Are you Really Listening, or Just Waiting to Talk?" Psychology Today, October 2016).

An Education World article on the traits of an effective principal can also apply to the role of Superintendent. One middle school principal stated, "Listening and understanding what you have heard is one of the most important traits. By listening to others, I can find ways to solve problems, help kids and parents, and support teachers." Effective listening as a Superintendent also enables you to assist the Board of Education (your boss) and the administrative team. Another principal said, "People do not always expect a principal to solve their problems. Many times, they just need someone who will listen to their concerns. An effective administrator knows when it is appropriate to shut up and just listen." An Illinois principal stated, "Listening conveys a caring attitude, and caring is a building block for trust" ("Good Principals: What Traits Do They Share?" Education World, 1999). Today's Superintendent needs to assist in developing a strong Board of Education, a strong mission and vision for the district, a strong administrative and district office team, strong principals, and a strong academic reputation for the district. In order to accomplish all of these things, a strong Superintendent must be a good listener.

The board, community, and employees know what they want and need in a leader. They pinpoint the behaviors and attitudes necessary to be the kind of Superintendent that they will follow to new levels of performance. When Superintendents take the time to understand what motivates and inspires their professional learning community (PLO), what their expectations are, and how to develop interpersonal relationships with them, then they can be the kind of leader that employees are willing to follow.

"When employees say they want their voices to be heard, they are really saying they want leaders who will not just hear them, but really listen to them. As employees seek more attention, feedback and support, leaders must become more mindful of individual needs so that we can more effectively inspire professional development and overall performance" (Glenn Llopis, "6 Ways Effective Listening Can Make You a Better Leader," Forbes, May 2013). This is especially true for Superintendents in order to support the overall health of the district.

As Superintendents, it is critical that we take the time to really listen. "Listening goes well beyond being quiet and giving someone your full attention" (Llopis). Otherwise, it is difficult to honestly know what our employees have on their minds and what is bothering them. Most importantly, they want to find out exactly how we are going to "get this school district out of this ineffective performance slump." Because of the "revolving door syndrome" in many school districts, some employees are just waiting until the next Superintendent arrives.

During the early stages of my superintendency, I (Elizabeth) hired an employee who had been a previous Superintendent. (In Illinois, the Superintendents recommend staff for hire.) This person served as a key staff member at the Cabinet level. At the start, our relationship was phenomenal: we consulted on a weekly basis, and the individual was invaluable. Over a few months, however, his demeanor changed; I observed that he was not as impactful and enthusiastic as he was originally. When his performance changed, as he intimidated support and certified staff, he negatively impacted our progress in the district. I met with him weekly, as I would meet with all Cabinet members in a group meeting once a week and hold individual meetings with key members. This time, I met with this employee to deliberately discuss what my coworkers (staff members) and I had noticed regarding his behavior. He responded, "I have some personal problems that prevent me from coming to work on time." He had been six months on the job and was now falling short on his attendance and other important tasks. He did not expose the personal problem—one of my expectations of my leadership teams' members and Cabinet staff is to leave personal problems out of the workplace. While I care about employees, individuals and their personal problems can take on a life of their own, if you allow it.

This individual feared for his job, especially because I had recommended him. I tossed and turned a little about this conversation with this employee, out of concern. On the other hand, I felt that I had not been a good listener. Perhaps I could have made an exception to the rule of not bringing personal stuff to the workplace. I thought long and hard about this case. I decided that I must use my common sense. After all, this individual was my right-hand person. Had I observed and listened to the signals and talked to him from the onset, maybe I could have intervened earlier. Instead, I waited until his job had become problematic. As I reflected on this case, I determined that I should have been more caring and a much better listener. After several conversations and improvement plans, I was determined to listen more deliberately next time.

His situation worked out, as life would have it; he was dealing with a very nasty divorce, and his wife had left him with several small kids. He was embarrassed, and the last thing he needed was to lose his job. My moral to this story is not to jeopardize the students that we are paid to serve, but rather continue to provide excellent service to our students and listen to this key staff member, and provide assistance to him for a designated amount of time in hopes that he will get his personal act together. If he is not able to get it together, then the next steps will be progressive discipline, including the possibility of termination.

Listening is never spelled out in the position description, but when Superintendents listen, they are in a much better position to lead. Having the reputation of being a great listener is a wonderful attribute. You are respected more when you listen. The one-size-fits-all approach does not work. People are different, and the workforce is different. Leaders must listen more in order to lead an "increasingly diverse and multigenerational workforce" (Llopis).

> **Elizabeth:** This is my 14th year in this urban school district, located about 30 miles south of Chicago. This is a district that my husband had the opportunity to serve as Superintendent before me. Because he had served as interim Superintendent prior to being offered the position, he turned down the offer largely due to the micro-management on the part of the board president. Other negative factors were involved, such as a dysfunctional Board of Education, lack of board training, poor management, funding deficits for years, a lack of confidence on the part of the state, lack of sufficient staff and of professional development for all staff, a large number of legal bills (because of not following staff contractual agreements), and frequent administrative turnover.
>
> I was approached by the board president at that time, who asked my husband if I would come to the district and "turn the district around." I did not realize at that time that I was called a "turn-around Superintendent." I guess that is a compliment—you decide. I had already served two other districts successfully, as evidenced by evaluations on the part of the board, community, staff, and parents. Because the district was in such disarray, my husband stated that "it would take God himself to turn the district around." After much prayer and thought, I decided that the only way to go was up! And I guess I can say the rest is history, as it did take God and a lot of really hard work. I started out on a listening tour and have remained a good listener even now. It has paid off for me.

Research was done (September 2005-June 2006) on the success of Superintendents across the nation who had been honored as outstanding by their state or national peers. Information was gathered "regarding the value of communication to increased student achievement and superintendent success." Seventeen superintendents were asked to participate by responding to open-ended questions in surveys and interviews. One question was, "List three to five skills you define as the most important to your success as a superintendent." "Every superintendent interviewed (100%) responded affirmatively when asked if communications plays a role in improving student achievement" (National School Public Relations Association [NSPRA], "Characteristics of Effective Superintendents").

Speaking to a group of visitors from across the state.

*Listening to the visitors who had several
great comments and great questions.*

*Listening as a part of a PLO
(Professional Learning Organization Meeting)*

M

MONEY MATTER

- *Money management should be considered a spiritual matter.*

- *Don't expect God to bail you out if you haven't included Him in your decisions.*

- *When you have dug yourself into a pit of debt, there's only one direction you can look: up.*

- *The only debt you can never repay is God's love for you. Work on paying all of the others with His help.*

- *God may not plan for you to be rich, but He certainly doesn't want you to be in debt.*

—Bruce & Stan, God is in the Hard Stuff

Money Matters

> *"You cannot serve both God and money."*
>
> *(Matthew 6:24 NIV)*
>
> *"The love of money is the root of all evil."*
>
> *(1 Timothy 6:10 KJV)*

Manage your money so students will achieve. You must set up procedures for managing all of the money that flows through the district, or it will get away from you. Many applicants for the position of Superintendent do not have fiscal experience, and neither do they have experience in money management. In many such cases, they have an experienced business manager on board.

All of the above notwithstanding, the candidate needs to know his or her budget well enough to know all of the sources of income flowing through the district. Who is authorized to spend what, and are adequate spending controls in place? Are there checks and balances? In all public school districts, there will be audits required by law. Even so, there have to be policies and administrative procedures in place that dictate how funds will be used and spent. This cannot be stressed enough. There have been so many Superintendents all over the country who have been fired because of money-related issues.

Many capable young Superintendents have lost their first job because they did not know where the "bleeding" was taking place. In recent years, we have noticed some of our colleagues have been removed in disgrace because they thought they could save funds by doing the roles of Superintendent and business manager simultaneously.

This has created problems in many districts. There is a strong need for checks and balances in order to keep certain functions separate and remove the temptation to "steal" because the person feels that he/she is so smart that no one will notice. Don't believe you can get away with it.

From my experience bringing three districts to a balanced budget, these are some of the areas where you need to look out for unnecessary spending as a new Superintendent:

1. Overstocking materials and supplies to the point that copy paper or construction paper has rotted.

2. Lack of procedure for the use of the attorney. Only approved people should speak to the attorney.

3. Checking all bills to be sure they are valid. I found that some video company had been billing one district for years, but it was not a legitimate company.

4. Overspending on substitutes because teachers have attendance problems. Work with the union and teachers to improve attendance.

5. Spending large sums of money sending large numbers of teachers to professional development when you can send just one or two who can come back and train others using the "Train the Trainer" model.

6. Spending large sums on vendors who have not served the district well. I worked with the staff to create large savings in just one year on contracted cleaning services, landscaping, food services, transportation services, and technology services, to name a few. (It is always smart to get at least three quotes, even on items that you do not have to go out to bid.)

7. Recruiting vendors to sponsor district events.

Our experience has shown us that when boards and individuals try to run the district, and do not know or understand their roles, as opposed to that of district Superintendent and staff, it results in poor management and morale, and the denial of the children's right to an education because the paid professionals find themselves distracted from their task by the lack of a coherent board that supports the teacher and administrators. One major problem facing urban blacks and other minority areas is the interference of some boards with the work of competent teachers led by knowledgeable administrators who are committed to spending the resources for the benefit of children and standing as advocates for children.

No matter the size of the school, the finances are critical to the success of the district. Talking with the district committee, the Chamber of Commerce, and the Board of Education about spending and budgeting, and how it is aligned to district goals and objectives, is a must in any district. Sharing work with our staff (including union members) and with our parents and elected officials is also important. Conduct monthly finance meetings, which can be chaired by an Board of Education member elected to conduct these meetings. Report out to the community each month about the finances. Maintaining a balanced budget has been extremely important to me, as we have managed to keep the budget balanced in my third district for over 13 years straight.

An article by David A. DeSchryver and Noelle Ellerson Ng ("District Spending Is About to Get a Lot More Transparent. Are You Ready?" Education Week, August 2018) discusses the issue of financial transparency as it relates to Superintendents:

It is time for superintendents to tackle a challenging conversation about how they allocate their limited financial resources—and how those decisions align with the core values of public education. Every Student Succeeds Act's fiscal transparency reporting requirement is a sleeper issue that will demand more of district leaders than just a change in how they communicate policy decisions with their communities. It will also prompt both school and district leaders to figure out how they manage productivity.

The idea of educational "productivity"—sometimes referred to as "performance-based investments" or "return on investment"—is not new. More than a decade ago, the credit rating agency Standard & Poor's tried to measure school productivity with their now-defunct School Matters service. The U.S. Department of Education took a stab at it in 2011, under the previous administration, with productivity guidance. The Center for American Progress got in on the action with its Return on Educational Investment report in 2014. Meanwhile, several states are beginning to explore the intersection of finance and academic performance at the school level. The list of initiatives goes on, but they have not required school leaders to meaningfully change the way they manage school spending relative to student outcomes.

The federal government has never asked this of districts, and few superintendents have thought through the mechanics of the work at the school level. Hard questions are cascading across the country: What to do with shared school costs? What about centrally purchased items? Do existing charts of accounts adequately capture the information required by law? All of these are sticky questions that administrators must soon resolve....

If the allocations seem to contradict the district's stated objectives, what will be done to adjust the investment strategy? The earlier that district leaders begin to pay attention to these matters, the less disruptive the new reporting and transparency will be for school and district staff faced with new questions from the public.

Over the long term, the new expenditure reporting requirements will push superintendents to be more strategic about managing productivity. This new transparency will make it easier for the public to investigate the relationship between academic and financial data.

Upon accepting the superintendency, I knew from the beginning that I had the difficult job of balancing the budget. This is a problem in many low-functioning districts for reasons such as:

- Revolving door of Superintendents
- Incompetent staff
- Lack of qualified business manager
- Lack of focus on spending
- Lack of spending plan
- Lack of vision for using district funds
- Lack of checks and balances
- Lack of policies and procedures
- Micromanaging on the part of the Board of Education

The list goes on and on. "No one is watching the store," so to speak. As Superintendents, we must be certain we are doing our best, spending wisely, and being good stewards of the community's taxpayer dollars. Funding is not just a conversation with the Superintendent and the Board of Education; funding and spending is a topic in all committee agendas, and the budget will always be on the agenda for weekly Cabinet meetings. (Little tip: Monday is a good day for Cabinet meetings because it is the first working day of the week.)

A proven success for us is to look at what funds we have from the state and look at the grant funds, especially our largest grant funder. I also examine all other grants, like special education and bilingual grants. It is critical that a smart Superintendent must look to get competitive and non-competitive grant funds. This approval has allowed me (Elizabeth) to balance three school district budgets in my first year as Superintendent in each district. If you are thinking programs must have been cut, that's not the case. In most instances, the money was always there for students in the district. It was usually an issue of not knowing how to manage old and new funds.

Many Superintendents are not successful because they never learned how to budget and are lacking skills needed in the finance area. Your short-range plan as a new Superintendent must include getting on top of the fiscal situation. You cannot be lured into holding on to staff who are dysfunctional. If there is not a need for that individual, it does not matter that the person has been there however many years. On another note, because you are a new Superintendent, everybody wants you to hire someone, but you must be brave. You cannot get caught in that trap. I can understand now why many boards will conduct a national search in order to get someone who has no connection to anyone in the community.

> **Elizabeth:** The record will show that during my tenure as Superintendent in my third district, with the support of a unified board, the district received much recognition for our accomplishments, including building funds for the district ranging from private foundations to national, state, and local grants. A few noteworthy accomplishments included:

- Higher achievement of our graduates

- Remaining fiscally sound with financial recognition every year for 13 consecutive years

- An annually expanding reserve

- Built a new middle school facility and paid in full

- Paid off debt from previous boards and Superintendent

- Raised reserve (over my tenure of 13 years) to over $21 million.

A few advantages of being a Superintendent?
- Higher salary and benefits; greater retirement benefits
- Variety in the day of a Superintendent, with constantly shifting priorities

- Control over the direction of the district—being prepared offers you the opportunity to see students excel on your watch

A few challenges?

- Budgeting and funding shortfalls
- If test scores decline or teacher satisfaction is low, it is on your watch
- Finessing negativity from parents and the community

On the issue of finances, Derrick Meador (ThoughtCo, 2019) writes:

The primary role of any superintendent is to develop and maintain a healthy school budget. If you are not good with money, then you will likely fail as a school superintendent. School finance is not an exact science. It is a complicated formula that changes from year to year especially in the realm of public education. The economy almost always dictates how much money is going to be available for the school district. Some years are better than others, but a superintendent must always figure out how and where to spend their money.

The toughest decisions a school superintendent will face are in those years of deficit. Cutting teachers and/or programs is never an easy decision. Superintendents ultimately have to make those tough decisions to keep their doors open. The truth is that it isn't easy and making cuts of any kind will have an impact on the quality of education the district provides. If cuts must be made, the superintendent must examine all options thoroughly and ultimately make cuts in the area where they believe the impact will be the least.

"Manage problems or they will manage you."
—Elizabeth H. Reynolds

FINANCIAL RECOGNITION

Under our leadership, we have balanced our district's fund balances consecutively and significantly maintained balanced budgets over 20 years.

ESTIMATED FINANCIAL PROFILE SUMMARY
(Go to the following website for reference to the Financial Profile)
www.isbe.net/sfms/p/profile.htm

District Name: Calumet Public School District 132
District Code: 07-016-1320-02
County Name: Cook

1. Fund Balance to Revenue Ratio:

Total Sum of Fund Balance (P8, Cells C81, D81, F81 & I81)	Funds 10, 20, 40, 70 + (50 & 60 if negative)	Total	8,910,403.00	Ratio	Score	4
Total Sum of Direct Revenues (P7, Cell C8, D8, F8 & I8)	Funds 10, 20, 40, & 70,		12,328,396.00	0.723	Weight	0.35
Less: Operating Debt Pledged to Other Funds (P8, Cell C54 thru D74)	Minus Funds 10 & 20		0.00		Value	1.40
(Excluding C:D57, C:D61, C:D65, C:D69 and C:D73)						

2. Expenditures to Revenue Ratio:

Total Sum of Direct Expenditures (P7, Cell C17, D17, F17, I17)	Funds 10, 20 & 40	Total	11,794,638.00	Ratio	Score	4
Total Sum of Direct Revenues (P7, Cell C8, D8, F8, & I8)	Funds 10, 20, 40 & 70,		12,323,396.00	0.957	Adjustment	0
Less: Operating Debt Pledged to Other Funds (P8, Cell C54 thru D74)	Minus Funds 10 & 20		0.00		Weight	0.35
(Excluding C:D57, C:D61, C:D65, C:D69 and C:D73)						
Possible Adjustment			0		Value	1.40

3. Days Cash on Hand:

Total Sum of Cash & Investments (P5, Cell C4, D4, F4, I4 & C5, D5, F5 & I5)	Funds 10, 20 40 & 70	Total	8,890,442.00	Days	Score	4
Total Sum of Direct Expenditures (P7, Cell C17, D17, F17 & I17)	Funds 10, 40 divided by 360		32,762.88	271.35	Weight	0.10
					Value	0.40

4. Percent of Short-Term Borrowing Maximum Remaining:

Tax Anticipation Warrants Borrowed (P25, Cell F6-7 & F11)	Funds 10, 20 & 40	Total	0.00	Percent	Score	4
EAV x 85% x Combined Tax Rates (P3, Cell J7 and J10)	(.85 x EAV) x Sum of Combined Tax Rates		3,435,693.31	100.00	Weight	0.10
					Value	0.40

5. Percent of Long-Term Debt Margin Remaining:

Long-Term Debt Outstanding (P3, Cell H37)		Total	4,225,768.00	Percent	Score	2
Total Long-Term Debt Allowed (P3, Cell H31)			6,299,919.97	32.92	Weight	0.10
					Value	0.20

Estimated 2016 Financial Profile Designation: **RECOGNITION**	Total Profile Score:	3.80 *

* Total Profile Score may change based on data provided on the Financial Profile
Information, page 3 and by the timing of mandated categorical payments. Final score will be
calculated by ISBE.

M

ESTIMATED FINANCIAL PROFILE SUMMARY
(Go to the following website for reference to the Financial Profile)
www.isbe.net/sfms/p/profile.htm

District Name: Calumet Public School District 132
District Code: 07-016-1320-02
County Name: Cook

1. Fund Balance to Revenue Ratio:

Total Sum of Fund Balance (P8, Cells C81, D81, F81 & I81)	Funds 10, 20, 40, 70 + (50 & 60 if negative)	**Total** 9,679,307.00	**Ratio** 0.766	**Score** 4
Total Sum of Direct Revenues (P7, Cell C8, D8, F8 & I8)	Funds 10, 20, 40, & 70,	12,640,106.00		**Weight** 0.35
Less: Operating Debt Pledged to Other Funds (P8, Cell C54 thru D74)	Minus Funds 10 & 20	0.00		**Value** 1.40
(Excluding C-D57, C-D61, C-D65, C-D69 and C-D73)				

2. Expenditures to Revenue Ratio:

Total Sum of Direct Expenditures (P7, Cell C17, D17, F17, I17)	Funds 10, 20 & 40	**Total** 11,871,200.00	**Ratio** 0.939	**Score** 4
Total Sum of Direct Revenues (P7, Cell C8, D8, F8, & I8)	Funds 10, 20, 40 & 70,	12,640,106.00		**Adjustment** 0
Less: Operating Debt Pledged to Other Funds (P8, Cell C54 thru D74)	Minus Funds 10 & 20	0.00		**Weight** 0.35
(Excluding C-D57, C-D61, C-D65, C-D69 and C-D73)			**Value** 0	**Value** 1.40
Possible Adjustment:				

3. Days Cash on Hand:

Total Sum of Cash & Investments (P5, Cell C4, D4, F4, I4 & C5, D5, F5 & I5)	Funds 10, 20 40 & 70	**Total** 9,641,453.00	**Days** 292.38	**Score** 4
Total Sum of Direct Expenditures (P7, Cell C17, D17, F17 & I17)	Funds 10, 20, 40 divided by 360	32,975.56		**Weight** 0.10
				Value 0.40

4. Percent of Short-Term Borrowing Maximum Remaining:

Tax Anticipation Warrants Borrowed (P25, Cell F6-7 & F11)	Funds 10, 20 & 40	**Total** 0.00	**Percent** 100.00	**Score** 4
EAV x 85% x Combined Tax Rates (P3, Cell J7 and J10)	(.85 x EAV) x Sum of Combined Tax Rates	3,443,618.78		**Weight** 0.10
				Value 0.40

5. Percent of Long-Term Debt Margin Remaining:

Long-Term Debt Outstanding (P3, Cell H37)		**Total** 3,915,795.00	**Percent** 37.90	**Score** 2
Total Long-Term Debt Allowed (P3, Cell H31)		6,305,906.14		**Weight** 0.10
				Value 0.20

Total Profile Score: 3.80 *

Estimated 2017 Financial Profile Designation-RECOGNITION

* Total Profile Score may change based on data provided on the Financial Profile Information, page 3 and by the timing of mandated categorical payments. Final score will be calculated by ISBE.

M

ESTIMATED FINANCIAL PROFILE SUMMARY

(Go to the following website for reference to the Financial Profile)

https://www.isbe.net/Pages/School-District-Financial-Profile.aspx

District Name: Calumet Public School District 132
District Code: 07-016-1320-02
County Name: Cook

1. Fund Balance to Revenue Ratio:

Total Sum of Fund Balance (P8, Cells C81, D81, F81 & I81)	Funds 10, 20, 40, 70 + (50 & 80 if negative)	**Total** 10,168,565.00	**Ratio** 0.793	**Score** 4 / **Weight** 0.35	
Total Sum of Direct Revenues (P7, Cell C6, D8, F8 & I8)	Funds 10, 20, & 70,	12,815,669.00		**Value** 1.40	
Less: Operating Debt Pledged to Other Funds (P8, Cell C54 thru D74)	Minus Funds 10 & 20	(117,903.00)			
(Excluding C-D57, C-D61, C-D65, C-D69 and C-D73)					

2. Expenditures to Revenue Ratio:

Total Sum of Direct Expenditures (P7, Cell C17, D17, F17, I17)	Funds 10, 20 & 40	**Total** 12,326,411.00	**Ratio** 0.962	**Score** 4 / **Adjustment** 0 / **Weight** 0.35	
Total Sum of Direct Revenues (P7, Cell C8, D8, F8, & I8)	Funds 10, 20, 40, & 70,	12,815,669.00			
Less: Operating Debt Pledged to Other Funds (P8, Cell C54 thru D74)	Minus Funds 10 & 20	(117,903.00)		**Adjustment** 0	
(Excluding C-D57, C-D61, C-D65, C-D69 and C-D73)					
Possible Adjustment:		0		**Value** 1.40	

3. Days Cash on Hand:

Total Sum of Cash & Investments (P5, Cell C4, D4, F4, I4 & C5, D5, F5 & I5)	Funds 10, 20 40 & 70	**Total** 10,135,630.00	**Days** 296.04	**Score** 4 / **Weight** 0.10	
Total Sum of Direct Expenditures (P7, Cell C17, D17, F17 & I17)	Funds 10, 20, 40 divided by 360	34,240.03		**Value** 0.40	

4. Percent of Short-Term Borrowing Maximum Remaining:

Tax Anticipation Warrants Borrowed (P25, Cell F6-7 & F11)	Funds 10, 20 & 40	**Total** 0.00	**Percent** 100.00	**Score** 4 / **Weight** 0.10	
EAV x 85% x Combined Tax Rates (P3, Cell J7 and J10)	(85 x EAV) x Sum of Combined Tax Rates	3,306,234.03		**Value** 0.40	

5. Percent of Long-Term Debt Margin Remaining:

Long-Term Debt Outstanding (P3, Cell H37)	**Total** 3,686,421.00	**Percent** 43.39	**Score** 2 / **Weight** 0.10	
Total Long-Term Debt Allowed (P3, Cell H31)	6,508,743.64		**Value** 0.20	

* Total Profile Score may change based on data provided on the Financial Profile Information, page 3 and by the timing of mandated categorical payments. Final score will be calculated by ISBE.

Total Profile Score: 3.80 *

Estimated 2018 Financial Profile Designation:	RECOGNITION

ESTIMATED FINANCIAL PROFILE SUMMARY

(Go to the following website for reference to the Financial Profile)

https://www.isbe.net/Pages/School-District-Financial-Profile.aspx

District Name:	Calumet Public School District 132
District Code:	07-016-1320-02
County Name:	Cook

			Total	Ratio	Score	4
1. Fund Balance to Revenue Ratio:			13,517,136.00	0.946	Weight	0.35
Total Sum of Fund Balance (P8, Cells C81, D81, F81 & I81)	Funds 10, 20, 40, 70 + (50 & 80 if negative)		14,294,121.00		Value	1.40
Total Sum of Direct Revenues (P7, Cell C3, D8, F8 & I8)	Funds 10, 20, 40, & 70,		0.00			
Less: Operating Debt Pledged to Other Funds (P8, Cell C54 thru D74)	Minus Funds 10 & 20					
(Excluding C:D57, C:D61, C:D65, C:D69 and C:D73)						
2. Expenditures to Revenue Ratio:			**Total**	**Ratio**	**Score**	**4**
Total Sum of Direct Expenditures (P7, Cell C17, D17, F17, I17)	Funds 10, 20 & 40		12,803,050.00	0.896	Adjustment	0
Total Sum of Direct Revenues (P7, Cell C8, D8, F8, & I8)	Funds 10, 20, 40, & 70,		14,294,121.00		Weight	0.35
Less: Operating Debt Pledged to Other Funds (P8, Cell C54 thru D74)	Minus Funds 10 & 20		0.00	0	Value	1.40
(Excluding C:D57, C:D61, C:D65, C:D69 and C:D73)						
Possible Adjustment:						
3. Days Cash on Hand:			**Total**	**Days**	**Score**	**4**
Total Sum of Cash & Investments (P5, Cell C4, D4, F4, I4 & C5, D5, F5 & I5)	Funds 10, 20 40 & 70		13,522,419.00	380.22	Weight	0.10
Total Sum of Direct Expenditures (P7, Cell C17, D17, F17 & I17)	Funds 10, 20, 40 divided by 360		35,564.03		Value	0.40
4. Percent of Short-Term Borrowing Maximum Remaining:			**Total**	**Percent**	**Score**	**4**
Tax Anticipation Warrants Borrowed (P24, Cell F6-7 & F11)	Funds 10, 20 & 40		0.00	100.00	Weight	0.10
EAV x 85% x Combined Tax Rates (P3, Cell J7 and J10)	(.85 x EAV) x Sum of Combined Tax Rates		2,912,865.36		Value	0.40
5. Percent of Long-Term Debt Margin Remaining:			**Total**	**Percent**	**Score**	**3**
Long-Term Debt Outstanding (P3, Cell H37)			3,179,000.00	51.18	Weight	0.10
Total Long-Term Debt Allowed (P3, Cell H31)			6,512,140.03		Value	0.30

Total Profile Score: 3.90 *

Estimated 2019 Financial Profile Designation: RECOGNITION

* Total Profile Score may change based on data provided on the Financial Profile Information, page 3 and by the timing of mandated categorical payments. Final score will be calculated by ISBE.

M

ESTIMATED FINANCIAL PROFILE SUMMARY

(Go to the following website for reference to the Financial Profile)

https://www.isbe.net/Pages/School-District-Financial-Profile.aspx

District Name: Calumet Public School District 132
District Code: 07-016-1320-02
County Name: Cook

1. Fund Balance to Revenue Ratio:

Total Sum of Fund Balance (P8, Cells C81, D81, F81 & I81)	Funds 10, 20, 40, 70 - (50 & 80 if negative)	**Total** 17,265,868.00	**Ratio** 1.155	**Score** 4 **Weight** 0.35
Total Sum of Direct Revenues (P7, Cell C8, D8, F8 & I8)	Funds 10, 20, 40, & 70,	14,945,191.00		**Value** 1.60
Less: Operating Debt Pledged to Other Funds (P8, Cell C54 thru D74)	Minus Funds 10 & 20	0.00		

2. Expenditures to Revenue Ratio:

Total Sum of Direct Expenditures (P7, Cell C17, D17, F17, I17)	Funds 10, 20 & 40	**Total** 13,181,039.00	**Ratio** 0.882	**Score** 4 **Adjustment** 0
Total Sum of Direct Revenues (P7, Cell C8, D8, F8, & I8)	Funds 10, 20, 40 & 70,	14,945,191.00		**Weight** 0.35
Less: Operating Debt Pledged to Other Funds (P8, Cell C54 thru D74).	Minus Funds 10 & 20	0.00		
(Excluding C-D57, C-D61, C-D65, C-D69 and C-D73)				**Value** 1.40
Possible Adjustment:			0	

3. Days Cash on Hand:

Total Sum of Cash & Investments (P3, Cell C4, D4, F4, I4 & C5, D5, F5 & I5)	Funds 10, 20-40 & 70	**Total** 17,265,868.00	**Days** 471.56	**Score** 4 **Weight** 0.10
Total Sum of Direct Expenditures (P7, Cell C17, D17, F17 & I17)	Funds 10, 20, 40 divided by 360	36,614.00		**Value** 0.40

4. Percent of Short-Term Borrowing Maximum Remaining:

Tax Anticipation Warrants Borrowed (P24, Cell F6-7 & F11)		**Total** 0.00	**Percent** 100.00	**Score** 4 **Weight** 0.10
EAV x 85% x Combined Tax Rates (P3, Cell I7 and I10)	(.85 x EAV) x Sum of Combined Tax Rates	3,874,959.00		**Value** 0.40

5. Percent of Long-Term Debt Margin Remaining:

Long-Term Debt Outstanding (P3, Cell H37)		**Total** 2,963,000.00	**Percent** 55.84	**Score** 3 **Weight** 0.10
Total Long-Term Debt Allowed (P3, Cell H31)		6,709,870.78		**Value** 0.30

Total Profile Score: 3.90 *

Estimated 2020 Financial Profile Designation:	RECOGNITION

* Total Profile Score may change based on data provided on the Financial Profile Information, page 3 and by the timing of mandated categorical payments. Final score will be calculated by ISBE.

N

NURTURE AND NEVER QUIT

Nurture and Never Quit

> *"And, ye fathers, provoke not your children*
>
> *to wrath: but bring them up in the nurture*
>
> *and admonition of the Lord."*
>
> *(Ephesians 6:4 KJV)*

It is important for Superintendents to hire good staff. Working with an excellent staff is the key to having a great organization. This goal is important because as we hire good staff, we want them to grow. How can staff grow under our leadership? We must have a well-thought-out plan that involves developing our staff into great leaders. We want to offer data-driven, research-based professional development on at least a monthly basis for our staff. We want them to be recruited, trained, and remain with us. We do not want the Revolving Door Syndrome. We want staff who will say "I have found my place" and can retire from here. Our goal has been to hire tough, pay well, train often, and command excellence.

HOW DO I NURTURE?

Some successful ideas we have used are:

- Provide monthly half-day professional development sessions for all teachers and paraprofessionals throughout the school year.

- Provide a weekly Cabinet training meeting for all key administrative staff.

- Offer a two or three-day kick-off retreat at the beginning of the year for all key administrative staff.

- Provide a peaceful room for students and a separate peaceful room for staff

We plan and execute all professional development meetings. We offer "Book Reads" for the entire district and community. It is also a good idea to try to get your local mayor to get involved from time to time. The staff Peace Room we have provided has had soft music and massage chairs. It's always good to pamper your staff. Teachers and staff members are offered opportunities to earn additional funds by conducting professional developments for staff and by working on special academic projects. Our administrative team members now present sessions for other school districts.

NEVER QUIT

In sharing stories with teachers and young administrators who have aspirations for the superintendency, I find too many operate under the ancient fable that some children are unable to learn the expected curriculum at their grade level. Having embraced this philosophy, they accept segregating these children into groups that are not expected to learn. I believe a Superintendent's job is to demand that all children are challenged to demonstrate measurable academic growth. The teacher must demonstrate mastery of an assortment of strategies to move his/her pupils.

In my first superintendency, a special education teacher was concerned about how to ensure his students graduated with competence to be self-supporting. His strategy was to identify all of the skills and competencies a graduate needed and package that with an internship where the student was reinforced by working with an adult mentor. The student met the requirements for graduation and was offered a full-time job by the company where he served as an intern. Most of the students in this program met the requirements and graduated with the necessary skills to begin earning way above minimum wage at the time.

RIDING THE CIRCUIT

One of the jobs I held on my way to the principalship was a "circuit counselor." That was not the official nomenclature for the job but my own. My actual job was to cover the district's five junior high schools once per week to help the school counselors deal with "difficult" students, generally those who had problems in the classroom obeying their teachers or disrupting the classroom.

Once, a student was referred to me for counseling. At our appointment, I asked him to describe his behavior when the teacher sent him to the dean. His primary reply: "The teacher does not like me." I asked, "What were you doing?" He finally said he had gone to sharpen his pencil. I met the teacher, and he described the student as generally well-behaved and friendly, and said he got along with his peers. I asked him how he really felt about the student, and he replied that he really liked the student except when he disrupted the class. He added that the student was bright. In our next session, I related to the student that the teacher liked him but did not like it when he disrupted the class.

Harry's Reflections:

In Oakland, California, my mentor, Dr. Foster, who was superintendent advised his assistant superintendents to remember that one of our major roles was to create "disciples" who would carry on the work in future years. He encouraged us to identify and nurture those individuals who demonstrated leadership potential. This could be done by allowing these staff members interested in leadership to take on available district leadership opportunities. Their opportunities could include substituting for principals; taking on the role of summer school principal; leading curriculum committees; leading administrative study groups -changing the reporting and grading system in the school district may be an area that needed to be discussed.

In each district; each year we have organized an administrative leadership academy housed within the district. This has been a pretty big deal. The academy is advertised and applicants in the district are encouraged to apply. This program is competitive since we accept about 30 individuals each year. As superintendents; we have led this program. Some individuals are recommended by their supervisors; since each applicant is asked for 3 written references in order to be admitted in the program. The program also required everyone to complete a district related project; a project that may have been recommended by their supervisor or another leader in the same district. The purpose of the academy is to recruit; train and retain potential leaders at all levels- any staff member interested in learning about how to become an effective leader was considered. The concept of "growing your own" was the idea of grooming your own individuals in house since it became extremely difficult to find strong leaders who were also strong instructionally. Many principals that we interviewed wanted the title however did not want to visit the classrooms every day and work with teachers who were struggling. We did not need principals to sit in the office all day rather to get out and about the school going in and out of classrooms assisting teachers; making themselves visible throughout the school and the community. (inside the schools and on the school grounds)

The program is designed to motivate and encourage staff members. This is a year- long program; much like a college class; that includes a syllabus for the course. For 2 years; we had a joint agreement with one of the universities that allowed our staff members involved in the program to receive graduate college credit for their participation in the academy. This was a real bonus for the participants.

Many of our graduates are currently serving as superintendents. One of These individuals stated that the leadership opportunities; including the chance to be involved in the leadership academy allowed her to grow to a level beyond her wildest dreams. Other graduates have stated that the leadership experiences in district allowed them to understand leadership on a move personal level.

> "Not everything that is faced can be changed, but
> nothing can be changed until it is faced."
> -James Baldwin

This is a copy of a framed certificate presented to Dr. Elizabeth H. Reynolds by a leader of a parent/community meeting group upon

❧A Good Superintendent ❧

A good Superintendent is one who shows grace under fire.....One whose loyalty is to the children.....One who never strikes with venom, only with fact, and her strikes are oh so Elegant.....One who listens and respects the needs of the parents, whose children she is responsible.....One who wastes no time with nonsense and stays focused on the path of educational bliss for all children.....One whose mission is to destroy educational failure.....and Annihilate the road to illiteracy based prison facilities awaiting our failed children.....One who makes no exceptions in this sacred war.....One who requires only High Expectations to enter her door....A Good Superintendent is......... Dr. Elizabeth Reynolds.....The answer to our children's resurrection from a state of illiterate death..... inflicted on them by incompetent leaders of a delicate system.....She is a God send.....the life breath that we've for so long awaited.....to save our children from Genocide..... Thank You ❧Dr. E. Reynolds❧

190

O

OPTIMISTIC

Optimistic

> *"Have I not commanded you? Be strong and courageous. Do not be frightened, and do not be dismayed, for the Lord your God is with you wherever you go." (Joshua 1:9 ESV)*

Working as a Superintendent, you will have many challenges. Boards of Education vary in number according to each state (seven in Illinois, nine in Tennessee, five in California), always an odd number in order to make sure you do not have tie votes. A quorum is always the majority of the board. For example, with seven board members, a quorum would be four members. As you know by now, all board meeting agendas must be posted, and this is a legal requirement.

The Superintendent is the one and only employee the Board of Education has. Many Boards of Education, or members of those boards, do not recognize that they have only one employee. What the Board of Education may not recognize is that the Superintendent's role is not a servant of individual board members, but he/she reports to the whole board as a collective group. When it works together in this fashion, that is a beautiful thing. The Board/Superintendent relationship should be like a beautiful marriage—no secrets, no surprises.

Harry's Reflections:

The Sequoia Union High School district located in Redwood City, California, was the most beautiful board I ever had. They knew the job, the way the whole thing should work out. During the process of offering me the job, they made it clear to me that they were not interested in running the district. They felt that the management and running of the district within the framework of board policy was my job. They also had a clear emphasis on open communication between them and me, between me and the community, and between me and the patrons.

Additionally, they were active salespersons for the district and talked it up. They took every opportunity to keep me informed about what they heard in the community. I also kept them informed about all aspects of the operations, some of which they might not have known about.

From the beginning of our relationship, we identified the most pressing issues and developed long-range and short-term goals designed to measure our progress. At the beginning of my tenure, the district was in the process of closing the only high school that was in a predominantly minority community. The plan was to reassign the predominantly minority population of Ravenswood High School to the remaining high schools. Though all kinds of efforts had been made to raise the number of nonwhite students attending Ravenswood, the district had not been successful. Eventually the number was raised, but not to the level the district had hoped. A number of white students did transfer because they were interested in what the board was trying to accomplish: a greater mix of the races. The positive was the quality and quantity of the progress that the board had made. I was so proud to be their Superintendent.

The San Francisco Peninsula is an upper-middle-class to middle-class community both in terms of socioeconomics and academic achievement. This resulted over time in the families that were having children being unable to afford housing on the peninsula. The population in our high schools therefore started to drop, and school sites that had been purchased in anticipation of growth became surplus, as well as having surplus space in some buildings. One of the solutions to this problem was closing Ravenswood and assigning those students to the remaining schools.

The optimism was when the district was growing. The board showed great wisdom and insight in purchasing vacant land, which was much cheaper at that time. During my tenure, California school districts that were deemed to have a rich tax base had their taxing ability for schools reduced or controlled until such time as other school districts that did not have such a tax base caught up (or were equalized). They were equalizing the tax base. We could buy things in our district that other schools could not buy. Talk about equality—there was none. Proposition 13 was designed as an equity issue, a way of equalizing support for schools. Illinois has dealt with the very same issue.

I was serving as Superintendent in a very optimistic district because my board and I worked extremely well together, and we were all optimistic. I had a very stable board that understood their role, and they were well informed. They were reelected often and were a very sophisticated board, and the district was sometimes referred to as a "sophisticated district." When you have that kind of board, you can accomplish, create, and do just about anything.

I served as a Superintendent for six years in that district, and I feel that I could still be there even today if I had not been lured away by a board member I had met in the South. He convinced me that I needed to come, and that I was the right person needed to accomplish something in his "problem district." It was the only move that I made as Superintendent that did not work out as I had hoped, and that was because I did not have a unified board. I was still optimistic, but I did not have the well-informed care of patrons and professionals who knew and identified what we needed to do. On the Peninsula, they knew how to get things done, while the district that I accepted had a huge amount of political friction and lot of political stuff. However, there is always a great amount of good that can be done in any district that you serve.

O

SAMPLE

Administrator's Handbook

Dr. Elizabeth H. Reynolds
Superintendent

OUR VISION STATEMENT

"In pursuit of academic excellence, the mission of our District is to form a partnership family, community, and the educational staff to develop academic, social, emotional and cultural needs of all students."

Table of Contents

August 7, 2017

Dear Colleague,

Welcome to the 2017-2018 school year! I am delighted to have you as a member of our District's leadership team. I am looking forward to working with you to make this another exceptional year. We again have the unique opportunity to work together to move our students to higher levels of achievement this year. We have the materials, training, skills, and knowledge to do so. I am sure that I can count on you.

Over a 2-day period, we will collaborate with other team members as we focus our attention on what we are about – teaching and learning for all students. You will connect again with peers to continue to build a common base of knowledge about what is working in the field to enhance student achievement. The 2-day sessions will focus on building the capacity of individual staff and schools to function as results-oriented, data-driven, professional learning communities. More importantly, you will have the chance to work with a team of like-minded professionals. I am asking that you come prepared by reading and internalizing the enclosed materials prior to the meeting.

We will meet in the Board Room on Monday, August 7 and Tuesday, August 8, 2017 from 8:30 a.m. until 3:00 p.m. Coffee/treats/lunch will be provided on both days.

Our theme will be The 5 Coaching Habits of Excellent Leaders. Please plan to contribute your unique insights and goodwill in order to create productive, enjoyable, shared experiences over the 2 days, as well as over the 2017-2018 school year.

Sincerely,
Dr. Elizabeth H. Reynolds
Superintendent

O

O

P

PERFORM WITH PURPOSE

Perform with Purpose

> *"So will I sing praise unto thy name*
> *for ever, that I may daily perform my vows."*
> *(Psalm 61:8 KJV)*

As a Superintendent, you must be clear about your purpose. Again, a Board of Education has only one employee, and that is the Superintendent. Board of Education members are elected officials and will usually hold their seat for up to four years. When new board members are elected, the priorities of the previous board can shift. A Superintendent must be prepared to listen to and work with the new board. Chaos and confusion can occur. However, one of the most important moves you can make is to host a special meeting to share past concerns and present and future initiatives, and to clarify expectations, board to staff and staff to board. Having a deliberate conversation and being allowed to offer a discussion regarding concerns on both sides is essential.

During Harry's considerable experience as a school administrator and as Superintendent of several school districts, I (Elizabeth) have had the opportunity to observe Superintendents and work productively with board members. During our own tenure as Superintendent of several districts, we have worked successfully with board presidents and members. In all of these situations, the relations were characterized by some important behavioral characteristics of the board members and presidents:

1. Everyone knew and understood their role

2. All board members were avid and active supporters and salesmen for the district

3. All observed the principle of "no surprises" and not trying to "set up" the Superintendent or principals in a public meeting

4. All members were well informed about programs to refer inquirers to Superintendent or staff when they did not know

5. Board of Education members respected each other and school staff

6. All board members knew the goals and objectives that drove the district and provided avid support to the district and schools by working together with the Superintendent and board colleagues

We had ground rules we adhered to in all Board/Superintendent meetings. During our tenure as Superintendent of any district, we have made a point of meeting regularly with the Board of Education president to discuss the agenda and any other issues of concern about the district. The purpose of these meetings is to keep the president informed so that he/she is able to speak with fidelity when talking about the district. This did not eliminate the fact that all information was still shared in a weekly update to the board. The rule that "ONE KNOWS, ALL KNOW" was memorialized and approved at a board meeting along with other Board/Superintendent agreements.

The question is why am I here as superintendent? Or stated another way, what is my real purpose? Years ago, the top person in the school district was called the headmaster. The person was a master teacher. His or her principle task or purpose was to give direction and focus to the education of the students assigned to him/her. This function was met by the person's development of goals and objectives with the teachers. This lead individual was responsible for assessing how well the teachers were teaching the goals and how well the students mastered what was being taught. Additionally; the headmaster would be responsible for keeping the board informed regarding the performance of the students.

The superintendent; synonymous with the headmaster has the responsibility of doing all that has been stated of the headmaster including a secondary function. This secondary function includes keeping the parents and community informed. As it relates to the performance of students; furthermore, this includes; what if any strategies would be implemented; if improvement is necessary.

The superintendent may be expected to participate in several service clubs in the community. These service club memberships are important because they are the one place where a superintendent would have access to most of the leaders of the community including elected officials. I (Elizabeth) joined the Rotary Club in one district and remained an active member while serving as superintendent. Having the title of superintendent; I gave monthly reports on the progress of the district at each monthly meeting. In another district; I joined the Chamber of Commerce and remained a member of the Chamber for the duration of my time in the district. I was involved in every fundraiser and every event held in that community including their Fall Fest, community parade and their Annual Themed Gala.

P

'Bless the future'

New Calumet SD 132 superintendent meets community, talks about her vision for the beleaguered district

By Kati Phillips
Staff writer

The superintendent hired to turn around troubled Calumet Park School District 132 spoke publicly for the first time Tuesday regarding her vision for the district.

Supt. Elizabeth Reynolds said in an eight-minute speech during a reception at the township senior center that she wants to create a child-centered district that is characterized by strong leaders, qualified teachers, parental involvement and high academic and behavioral expectations of students.

All students should be capable of attending college, more school time should be focused on high-level teaching and students should be monitored frequently for progress, she said.

"The list is not exhaustive, and there may be many other traits that can be added to the list. However, the ones I have mentioned are the most essential as we look toward accomplishing this great goal of making School District 132 an excellent school district," she said.

School board president Bill Connor told the crowd of about 50 staff members, parents and elected officials that the board endorses Reynolds' vision.

"This is a time to stop saying negative things about our (schools)," he said. "We need to not curse the future, but bless

District 132 is the first in the state to be defined as "systemically noncompliant" after six years on probationary status. An oversight board will be appointed before next school year to create and monitor implementation of long-term financial and academic plans.

Reynolds, who has hired a new set of district- and school-level administrators, said her vision should be compatible with that of the oversight board.

"They are about students. I am about students," she said.

Reynolds said a key step to enacting her vision is to train teachers. She plans to immerse them in research on the best ways to teach struggling students how to read and solve math problems.

The district also will introduce "positive behavior intervention strategies" this fall that will reward students for good conduct.

Reynolds earned her Ph.D. at Vanderbilt University and has been superintendent of Park Forest and Maywood schools. She was interim superintendent of District 132 from February to June 30, 2004.

Several parents and community members said they were encouraged by Reynolds' speech.

"If they would've kept her in the first place, we wouldn't be in this trouble," said Constance Carter, the mother

Art Vasy/Daily Southtown

New Calumet Park School District 132 Supt. Elizabeth Reynolds talks to the

P

Q

QUIETNESS

Quietness

> *"And the work of righteousness shall be peace,*
> *and the effect of righteousness quietness and*
> *assurance for ever." (Isaiah 32:17 KJV)*

The word of wise men is heard in quiet. One of the purposes of this book is to share our experiences along the path of becoming a school Superintendent. Our hope is some of these may empower you so that you may be a more powerful and effective educational leader.

Harry's Reflections:

I recall an occasion when my mentor very skillfully "worked the room." My mentor was an extremely bright man and very smooth. He was not being "slick"; he just had finesse. My mentor worked with a room full of "patrons" with whom he had agreed to meet to hear their concerns. As a novice associate, I watched my mentor listen quietly, warmly, friendly, and responsively until all questions had been asked and answered. The crowd dispersed with a warm invitation to join him in working to improve our schools for our children.

I learned from this encounter and many others like this:
- To listen quietly and with courtesy
- To invite the critics to join in working with us
- To maintain a warm, friendly posture—not hostile
- To thank the audience for coming and providing valuable input

Effective school districts with an effective Superintendent have a lot to be thankful for. This certainly does not happen overnight. In a district that has been ineffective for years, it takes an act of God to turn that district around. When a district has had years of incompetence, as Superintendent, you must come in with a strong vision of excellence and provide strong strategic leadership. You must be an expert in the area of teaching and learning, be able to change the district in a Professional Learning Organization, and have the capacity to work with staff in improving all aspects of the organization simultaneously:

1. Board of Education / Superintendent relationships
2. Teaching and learning
3. Human Resources
4. Building and grounds
5. Technology
6. Parent and community relationships and involvement

Elizabeth's Reflections:

In my third superintendency, the district was dysfunctional. Everything that could be wrong was wrong. I had heard about the district because it had been in the news for years with a huge amount of negative publicity. The Board of Education had a real negative reputation, and deservingly so. I needed a challenge.

This was a nice community in the south suburbs of Chicago. When I was asked to accept the position, I realized that since everything in the district was "broken," there was no way to go but up! The district needed to be fixed—the children deserved better. The community also deserved better. Through school improvement planning and good communities, I knew that I could make a positive difference.

Because this district had so many problems for so many years, an oversight committee was assigned to the district upon my arrival. An oversight committee is a committee that is sent from the state to fix a district that is totally dysfunctional. The purpose of the oversight is to work with the district in order to correct the differences and provide the assistance needed over a period of several years. The oversight committee stayed with us in the district for three years. The three-year stay was not necessary for me; the district was functioning as a good district within the first year. I welcomed the assistance, however, even though it was not needed. I knew the role then, and I still know the role of a good Superintendent.

Serving as superintendent; quietness means having the ability to listen to all manner of input and remain silent. Quietness is necessary in order to understand the complainer. On your board agenda there is an agenda item that says, "Public Comments." There must be an item of this sort on a board agenda because the public has the right to address the board at every board meeting. This allows all sorts of interesting statements; maybe unrelated to the agenda; to be presented during this segment of the board agenda The board is not required to respond to the questions or comments; yet many times individual novice board members or a novice superintendent may feel the need to get involved during this time rather than remaining quiet. This could lead to all kinds of chaos which prolongs a meeting unnecessarily.

As a superintendent; quietness is also essential even if during public comments a community resident decides he or she wants to be heard and begins to share a lot of information that is totally false or irrelevant. If the board President asks the superintendent to speak in order to clarify information; that would be the appropriate time for the superintendent to speak, otherwise the superintendent should remain quiet.

The Board of Education and I began the journey with a special Board of Education meeting. In that initial board meeting, we allowed a facilitator to work with us in enabling the Board of Education and Superintendent (myself) to come up with Board of Education/Superintendent Agreements (see the following pages).

Calumet PSD 132 Essential Board Process Agreements
8/26/17...Addendum-10/7/17...Revised 4/14/18

✓ **Placing items on the agenda**
- o The Board President and the Superintendent confer to generate the agenda for an upcoming board meeting.

- o The Board President and the Superintendent will identify a common meeting date/time for all "agenda-generating" meetings and these dates/times will be relayed to the Board, well in advance.

Deadline to Submit Agenda Requests
→→→→→→

- Any board member desiring to have an item considered for an upcoming board agenda should contact the Superintendent with an emailed "cc" to the Board President **no later than** the first, five (5) business days of each new month.

Required Content for Agenda Requests
→→→→→→

- Any board member desiring to have an item considered for an upcoming board agenda must include a summary of the desired item as it relates to the following criteria:
  - Identify the item/topic for agenda consideration.
  - Share the reason(s) for consideration of the item/topic.
  - Share the connection of the requested agenda item to specific, Board ends [i.e., a board goals(s), core value/belief(s), mission, and/or vision].

Allowances to Condense/Omit Agenda Requests
→→→→→→

- In each "agenda-generating" meeting, the Board President and Superintendent may condense repetitive agenda requests from multiple board members and omit requests unrelated to board ends [specifically, a board goals(s), core value/belief(s), mission, and/or vision].

Notification To Advance Agenda Requests
→→→→→→

- Following receipt of agenda requests from any board member (and prior to issuance of the agenda for board packet inclusion), the Superintendent will issue an email to the Board identifying all final agenda items that were confirmed for agenda placement at the "agenda-generating" meeting of the Board President and the Superintendent.

Agenda Position For Advanced Agenda Requests
→→→→→→

- Any item/topic that has been communicated to the Superintendent with an emailed "cc" to the Board President and met all other requirements for agenda consideration will advance for agenda placement for the subsequent, regularly scheduled board meeting under the heading/classification of "New Business."

Discussion On Advanced Agenda Requests
→→→→→→

- The requesting Board member will be responsible for explaining the reason the topic was included on the agenda;
  - The board member will be conscious of time to ensure meeting efficiency and honor any request from the presiding officer to conclude the presentation.

Board Agreements Page 1

- A board member desiring to relay information to the Board should relay the information to the district office **no later than** the end of the first week of each month. Meeting this deadline will ensure that the information is included in the Board packet for advance review;
    - If the information a board member desires to distribute is not submitted to the district office by the established deadline, the information will be included in the Board packet for the next month.
- A board member desiring to relay Board Development resources to the Board may opt to secure the resources in an envelope (one envelope for each board member) and place each envelope at the place setting where each board member sits for a board meeting.

✓ **Asking a Board-related Question and/or Requesting Information from the Superintendent**
  - o An individual board member may only request Board-related information from the Superintendent and any information relayed to the requesting board member is issued to all other board members.   [**One Knows; All Know** Philosophy]
  - o A request for information from a board member to the Superintendent should be issued **no later than** the Thursday of each week.
  - o The Superintendent must relay all requests from any board member to the Board via a list that is contained in the Superintendent's weekly update;

- (In the list of board member requests for information) The Superintendent will denote next to each information request whether the information is classified as "immediate compliance"—meaning that the information is *file-cabinet-ready* (see definition below) and the information can be quickly compiled/relayed **OR** "detailed compliance"—meaning that the information cannot be quickly compiled/relayed and it will entail *voluminous information* (see definition below);
    - Definition: *File-Cabinet Ready*—Information held by the central office in hard copy form **or** finalized information (i.e., not in need of manipulation by staff) within a computerized database that can be easily printed (i.e., a quick print).
    - Definition: *Voluminous Information*—Information a board member requests of the Superintendent that will entail manipulation of data by staff **or** information where the finished product entails a voluminous (in-depth) report(s) and/or research.

Q

✓ **Asking questions about upcoming agenda items**
  o A board member who has a question regarding an upcoming agenda item should contact the Superintendent with the inquiry **no later than** the Tuesday prior to the board meeting when the agenda will be utilized.

✓ **Communicating with members**
  o Compliance to the Open Meetings Act (OMA) and board policy

✓ **Communicating with staff**
  o A board member desiring to contact a staff member should contact the Superintendent, who will respond appropriately.
  o A board member should not initiate contact with staff, in the capacity of a board member without full Board authorization.
  o When a parent, who is elected as a board member, communicates with staff in the "parent role," this individual must verbalize that he/she is not present as a board member but a parent.
    • Adhere to board policy (i.e., follow the same steps as any other citizen who is a parent).
    • All inquiries/requests of the parent who was elected as a board member will pertain to specific matters involving his/her individual student(s).

✓ **Visiting the campus**
  o Adhere to board policy (8:30).
  o Each visiting board member should follow district and school security measures/procedures.
  o A parent, who is elected as a board member, and visits a campus should follow board policy, standard district/campus visit procedures, and appropriate board protocols.

✓ **Responding to complaints**
  GENERAL CONCERNS:
  o Listen to the citizen.
  o Acknowledge the concern(s) of the citizen.
  o Refer the citizen sharing a concern(s) to established board policy such as the Chain of Command
  o Refer a citizen needing district-related assistance to the district office phone number;
    • A board member will ensure equal treatment for all inquiring citizens by refraining from any bypass of the established Chain of Command and any related board policy.
  o (Based on the severity of the concern/issue shared by a citizen) Contact the Superintendent and share the concern/issue presented by the citizen.

Board Agreements Page 3

213

EMAILED CONCERNS:
- o Reply to the email by acknowledging receipt.
- o (Based on the severity of the concern/issue presented in the email) Forward the concerning email to the Superintendent.
- o The Superintendent will respond, accordingly.
- o The full Board will receive the concerning email and the reply of the Superintendent.

✓ **Communicating with the media**
- o The Board President, in consultation with the Superintendent, serves as the spokesperson of the Board with the media.

✓ **Communicating with the public**
- o The Board President, in consultation with the Superintendent, serves as the spokesperson of the Board with the public.

✓ **Conducting closed sessions**
- o What is discussed/occurs in closed session stays in closed session.

✓ **Participating during public forums**
- o Adhere to board policy.
- o The Board President will initiate the public participation section of a board meeting by reading a script detailing the expectations of the Board (for the public participation section of a board meeting).
- o The Board will not respond to inquiries/comments of a citizen addressing the Board.
- o The Superintendent will ensure responses are issued to citizen inquiries/comments, as directed by the Board.
- o Questions (excluding those containing sensitive information) posed by a citizen during the public participation section of a board meeting along with appropriate, district responses will be noted/listed on the district web site prior to the subsequent, regularly scheduled board meeting.

Q

Board Agreements Page 4

"Don't mix bad words with your bad mood

You will have many opportunities to change

your mood, but you will never get the chance to

replace words you have spoken"

- Anonymous

R

Results/Rewards

> *"Look to yourselves, that we lose not those things which we have wrought, but that we receive a full reward." (2 John 1:8 KJV)*

Elizabeth: Don't worry your head off thinking about negative people. This is a part of what happens in life. Sometimes for me, negative people make me sharpen my game: "I stay on my toes." "Haters made us greater." Failure is not in our vocabulary. In a position of Superintendent, you look around at all staff. When you assume the job as a new Superintendent, you may eventually end up terminating all of the top administrative team or Cabinet members, but you shouldn't do this all at the same time—being new, you need as much stability as possible. When you work closely with people, a lot is revealed. People do not have to tell you they are loyal; loyalty is revealed.

R What you want in a school district is results for students. You don't have to love me to work hard, and I don't have to love you. As Harry says, "this is not a love boat." In other words, stop trying to make people like you. Just do your job. This is what I tell staff, and it has paid off. After a national search with 119 applicants, I was hired as Superintendent in my first district, in Illinois.

After lengthy interviews with key movers and shakers, union officers, district office team, and the Parent Teacher Association, to name a few, the board shared their concern about the school site leaders. These were principals and assistant principals. Their concern was that their district had been known as a premier district, but it now had a reputation as a district that was struggling academically. My guarantee was to turn the district around into becoming a "spotlight" district again.

The board and I agreed that because there was no shortage of funds in any area, if principals and assistants could do the job, why wasn't it being done? Why was the district losing ground? I had a board composed of three women and four men. I loved the board, and they treated me extremely well. After signing my contract with, of course, lawyers involved, my attorney and the board's attorney came to a mutual agreement. I knew I had to deliver. I was confident, but not cocky. Confident because I knew I was trained well, and also because I was married to a seasoned Superintendent who had worked successfully as Superintendent in California. He had also been hired as the first black Superintendent in Chattanooga, Tennessee, which was a huge deal in that county.

My first district was a dream come true; the board president and I formed a great relationship, and the board was not into trying to micromanage me or the district. That was a real blessing. The district flourished and received accolades in all areas: the board, the community, the students, the schools, the administrators, and the Professional Development programs, to name a few. After five years in that district, I resigned to take over a much larger district in Illinois. That was a mistake: the much larger district was hugely political, and it lacked the necessary funds to provide the kind of materials, supplies, and services needed to educate students at high levels. This tough experience allowed me to become a better Superintendent.

HARRY'S ACCOMPLISHMENTS IN CHATTANOOGA, TENNESSEE

1. Initiated a close working relationship with the College Board to strengthen our high school curriculum and increase students taking AP classes.

2. According to regular audits, the district was more than fiscally sound for the nine years of my tenure.

3. To affect the changes identified, we sought and received fiscal and other support form the following organizations:

    -   Lyndhurst Foundation

    -   McConnell Clark Foundation

    -   National Science Foundation (math and science)

    -   National Academy Foundation for mentoring high school students and exposing them to the world of work

    -   Little Debbie Corp.

4. We converted surplus school buildings to different successful models: Paideia schools, Montessori schools, Direct Instruction schools (very controversial schools), 21st Century Preparatory School, and other very different schools. However, all schools were charged with the responsibility of improving the lives of all students in the community. All schools had a community-wide focus.

5. We began training staff for the implementing of a K-12 practice guidance program designed to address and work with student issues earlier, before they interfere with the educational process.

One of the great blessings an aspiring Superintendent can hope for is to have competent, creative, and committed administrative staff. I have often been blessed over my many years with highly competent team players who made the team look good. A number of my colleagues who served with me have moved on to become successful Superintendents, while others finished their careers in the job they loved the most. One of the most helpful business managers I had the privilege of working with served the Chattanooga School District before my tenure and continued until the district was consolidated with Hamilton County Schools. Bill was a loyal colleague who kept me informed and who was often requested statewide to help other districts or even state committees. Several years ago, Bill and his wife got hooked on diving—he then started talking about retiring. I did not have the opportunity to thank him for his service to the children of Chattanooga

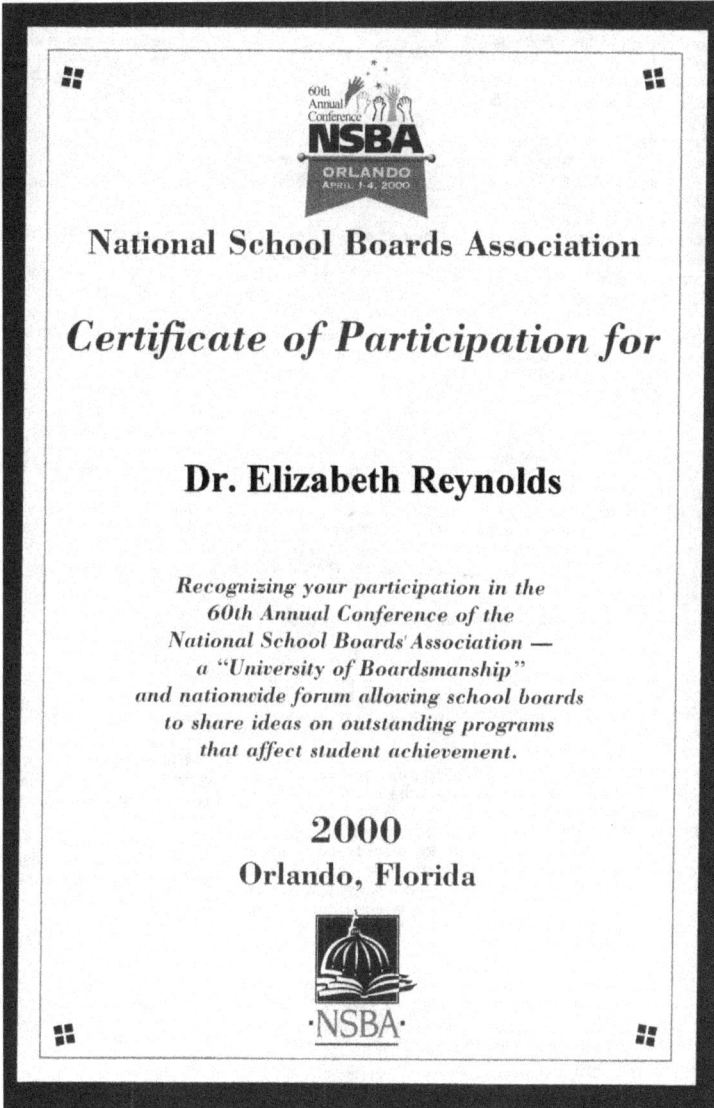

National School Boards Association

Certificate of Participation for

Dr. Elizabeth Reynolds

*Recognizing your participation in the
60th Annual Conference of the
National School Boards Association —
a "University of Boardsmanship"
and nationwide forum allowing school boards
to share ideas on outstanding programs
that affect student achievement.*

2000
Orlando, Florida

·NSBA·

Test scores rise in Dist. 89

BY JOHN HUSTON
STAFF WRITER

District 89 has posted increases in reading and math on the Illinois Standards Achievement Test.

The average scores across the Maywood-Melrose Park district's 10 schools showed marked improvements in most grade levels, except for third- and eighth-grade reading where performance stayed at the same level as last year.

"I think last year paid off for our students," said Superintendent Elizabeth Reynolds, who brought the Direct Instruction reading and Saxon math programs with her to District 89 when she was hired in June 2002.

Mathematics scores districtwide showed the biggest gains.

Third-graders scored an average of 58.1, compared to 49 the year before.

Fifth-graders increased their average score on the math section from 30 in 2002 to 52 this year; and eighth-graders posted an average math score of 24.8, compared to 16 in 2002.

Reading scores showed slower improvements.

	2001	2002	2003
Grade 3			
Reading	33	36	36
Math	45	49	58
Grade 5			
Reading	27	26	34
Math	28	30	52
Grade 8			
Reading	41	45	45

School District 89 test scores

Test scores increased at Maywood-Melrose Park School District 89 last year. Nonetheless, eight of the district's 10 schools will remain on the state's Academic Warning List.

Source: Maywood-Melrose Park School District 89   Pioneer Press / chc

Third-graders in District 89 averaged a 35.8 on the reading section, a slight decline from their average of 36 last year. Fifth-graders moved from 26 on the reading test to 33.9 this year. Eighth-graders posted a slight increase — from 45 to 45.4.

Even the categories that appeared to level off were signs of improvement over past declines, Reynolds said.

"We stopped the bleeding," Reynolds stated.

Grady Rivers Jr., the District 89 School Board president, voiced concern over the lack of improvement on the reading test.

"We were very happy about the Saxon math scores, but we were a little disappointed by the reading scores," he said. "I thought the reading numbers would be better, but I am very happy about the overall improvements and I believe we are on the right path."

Rivers and the slate of candidates who took seats on the board with him in April have pushed to reduce the Direct Instruction program in favor of a balanced literacy program.

(Continued on page 8)

■ Test scores Continued from page 5

Saxon Math will continue to be the district's mathematics curriculum.

Sue Carter, who was promoted from principal at Stevenson School to director of school site operations this year, said the new reading program, used in conjunction with Direct Instruction, is a positive step.

"I think our reading program will expand on what we had last year and add to it," she said.

Eight of District 89's 10 schools are on the state's Academic Warning List.

"With the improvements we will make with the curriculum this year, we are on the right path to getting off the Warning List," Rivers said.

Washington School in Maywood showed significant improvements, Reynolds noted.

On the 2003 reading test, 50 percent of the school's third-graders met or exceeded state standards in reading compared with just 18 percent in 2002.

Last year, only one of the two district schools not on the Warning List, Jane Addams School in Melrose Park, was capable of offering choice to students at failing schools — part of the No Child Left Behind Act.

This year, Stevenson School in Melrose Park will also be able to house students from failing schools who opt for the choice program.

On the 2003 Terra Nova test, which measures how close a student performs academically compared to his or her grade level, all but one grade level at Stevenson performed at or above the standard for their grade.

The scores, broken down by school and grade level, can be used to provide more specifically focused academic programs, Reynolds said.

"If there's a class level at one school lagging, just as a surgeon, we're going to pinpoint that," she said. "We're not going to give up and we're not going to slow the pace."

R

220

by Denise Faris

Curriculum maps chart journey

Denise Faris is public information coordinator for Park Forest-Chicago Heights School District 163.

eachers in Park Forest-Chicago Heights School District 163 have developed curriculum maps to clearly chart students' journey through eight years of elementary school and ensure increased academic achievement.

"It was a massive undertaking, but the district now has curriculum maps for math and science in place. Social science is the next area we'll map," said Beacon Hill Primary Center teacher Barbara Ruggles. "The maps are very specific. They detail for each grade level, on a monthly basis, the knowledge and skills that students should have mastered. While the maps increase teachers' accountability to their students and their parents, they also support greater efficiency in the classroom."

Under the leadership of Superintendent Elizabeth Reynolds, the maps were developed by teachers from all of the District's schools during the last school year and during summer break. Input also was sought from high school faculty members to ensure that District 163's eighth grade graduates were well prepared for the high school curriculum. University staff members, parents, and other community members also were part of the mapping process.

Teachers from kindergarten through eighth grade outlined for each curricular area the content that must be covered, when it must be addressed during the school year, the major skills which must be mastered, and when those skills must be mastered. This data formed the basis of the curriculum maps which specify what is to be covered in the classroom August through June.

No more gaps

"The math map, which was in place during the last school year, is based on the Illinois standards and on those set by the National Council of Teachers of Mathematics (NCTM)," said Beacon Hill faculty member Gordon Kridner. "The map is sequential and developmental so that one month's lesson is based on the previous month."

Superintendent Reynolds said the curriculum maps were important elements in achieving the District's first goal of increased academic success for all students.

"The mapping process eliminated gaps and repetitions in the curriculum," said Reynolds. "The maps help our teachers because they show them what to teach and when to teach it. The district, furthermore, provides the faculty members with the proper training so they are skillful instructors. The maps provide the what, the professionals determine the how."

Reynolds went on to say all district teachers have been trained in the mapping process. In turn, Dr. Reynolds and district staff members

Math Map

Social Studies Map

Direct *Instruction* **Profiles of Success**

Reading Scores Multiply Districtwide

The Challenge

Park Forest-Chicago Heights School District 163, located 40 minutes south of Chicago in the villages of Park Forest and Chicago Heights, had a history of poor performance on state and national tests. Its student population was 65% economically disadvantaged and 72% low income. Seeking profound change, the district carefully researched and examined other schools using **Direct Instruction (DI)**.

A Fresh Start

Under the direction of Superintendent Dr. Elizabeth H. Reynolds, **Direct Instruction** programs were implemented in six Pre-K–8 schools, serving a total of 2,200 students, during the 1998-99 school year. J/P Associates – a consulting group that provides professional development and hands-on assistance to schools implementing **DI** programs – worked with the district on the implementation.

Results in the first year alone showed improvement overall from younger to older students. The district's Terra Nova Assessment data shows that before **DI** was implemented, students in Grade 1 tested at the 48 National Curve Equivalent (NCE). After two years in the **DI** *Reading Mastery* program, scores soared to the 65.6 NCE. Similar results were achieved with Grades 2-8.

The Impact

Park Forest students in Grades 2-3 are involved in the Reading is Fundamental (RIF) program, and have a yearly opportunity to select books provided within this federally funded program. Within one year of beginning the **DI** program, the students' selection of books moved to a higher level, and additional books had to be purchased in the program to meet student needs.

Hope for the Future

"**Direct Instruction** has made a huge difference in the way our students are performing," said Dr. Reynolds. "Our students are now reading well and feel more confident about reading to any audience. Parents also are extremely pleased about the difference they can see in their children. Looking ahead, we can see elementary students who should be fully prepared for any high school or college across the country."

Profile Your Own Success

For additional information on SRA/McGraw-Hill's **Direct Instruction** programs, please contact us toll-free at 1-888-SRA-4543 and visit our web site at www.sra4kids.com.

R

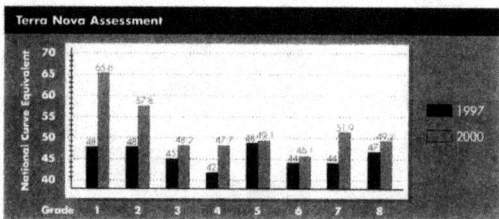

SRA McGraw-Hill

The results are proven, the possibilities endless.

A Division of The McGraw-Hill Companies

3. Building Trauma-Sensitive Systems Within Schools

Calumet Park School District 132 Results
Discipline

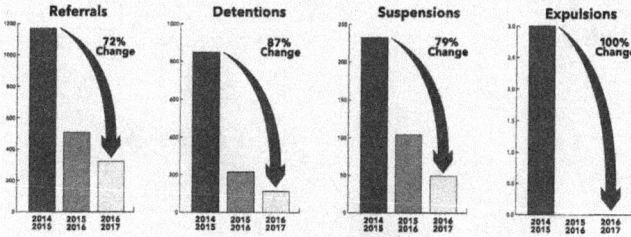

Academic outcomes
Students made statistically significant gains in English and Math across all grades K-8 in years one and two, correlated with the Partnership's work.

Resilience brain research is applicable everywhere but holds particular promise if applied consistently and broadly for children growing up in poverty. This means changing school environments, because, as trauma-sensitive schools expert Susan Cole notes, "schools are children's communities."

Adapting or redesigning schools, however, can be a long and very challenging process. Public schools in high-poverty districts are often hectic environments—struggling to keep up with day-to-day operations, budget constraints, changing regulations and mandates, and high turnover in leadership and personnel. School staff often experience secondary trauma or are surviving their own trauma and need care themselves.

The Partnership has engaged in a process that "meets districts and schools where they are," working collectively with school and community partners to create trauma-sensitive and resilient communities of care for students, parents, and staff. The process is predicated on systems change and takes a patient, capacity-building approach to changing school and classroom culture.

The core elements of the Partnership's approach to capacity-building are covered in the following sections:

- Assessing Readiness
- Identifying a Cadre of Leaders
- Organizing Structures That Can Drive Change and Learning
- Using the Structure for Power and Action
- Overcoming Real-World Resistance
- Using Data and Learning

Assessing Readiness

Readiness is an important element to consider when selecting school or district partners for a resilience initiative. A school or district's readiness will play a big role in its level and rate of success. When choosing its initial districts, the Partnership considered need along with the following readiness factors:

- *Collaborative relationships* between what the Consortium for Educational Change (a partner in the work) terms the "three anchors": the board of education; administration, including the superintendent; and teachers, particularly the union representative or a representative group.[8]

- A *culture* that values social-emotional learning: In the Southland, several participating districts worked

R

EDUCATION WEEK

American Education's Newspaper of Record — Volume XIV, Number 41 · August 2, 1995 — © 1995 Editorial Projects in Education / $3.00

Board Relaxes Bilingual-Ed. Policy in Calif.

Advocates Worry Vote Is Signal of Backlash

By Lynn Schnaiberg

The California board of education has given school districts more flexibility in how they teach students who speak little or no English, a move that may discourage the use of bilingual education in the state with more such students than any other in the nation.

At the same time that the board was debating the policy, wrangling over credentialing rules for teachers of limited-English-proficient students was pointing up sharp divisions on the issue among California teachers.

And Delaine Eastin, a former Democratic Assembly member who was elected the state schools superintendent last year, has come under fire from some bilingual-education advocates. They view her support of the state board's new policy—and some of her reported comments on bilingual education—as a letdown.

The developments show that the politically charged debate over how best to educate California's 1.2 million L.E.P. students—who make up one quarter of its enrollment—is very much alive.

Some national observers suggest that the events in California dramatize a larger backlash against bilingual education.

"Bilingual education is very clearly under attack in many other quarters," said James J. Lyons, the executive director of the National Association for Bilingual Education.

Local Flexibility

The California state board unanimously adopted the new policy at its July 14 meeting after months of public hearings and deliberations. It is a far cry from the original proposal floated last year, which would have emphasized that native-language instruction is not required. Some advocates of bilingual education said that draft would have effectively dismantled such programs and violated state law. (See *Education Week*, Dec. 14, 1994.)

While the state's bilingual-education law was allowed to expire in 1987, its language provided that its "general purposes" would

Continued on Page 21

Beyond City Limits

Last year, voters in Chattanooga, Tenn., voted to give up their school system and consolidate with the Hamilton County schools. But rather than just merge their systems, educators are working to craft an entirely new one that draws on the successes of both. Helping steer the effort are Superintendents Harry J. Reynolds of Chattanooga, left, and Don Loftis of Hamilton County, shown above at the downtown aquarium that symbolizes the city's rebirth. *See Story, Page 32.*

Bill To Push Block Grant For Education

Measure Would Allow Private School Vouchers

By Mark Pitsch
Washington

Key members of the House education committee are drafting legislation that would fold 11 federal education programs, including major initiatives such as Goals 2000, into a $1.4 billion block grant designed to spur reforms.

The proposal being designed by the panel's Republican leaders would share a central feature of the Clinton Administration's Goals 2000 strategy—a requirement that states and school districts adopt challenging academic-performance standards and assessments with which to measure students' progress toward meeting them.

The bill would also allow, for the first time, the use of federal education funds for voucher programs that include private schools.

The legislation, which is far from complete and will not be introduced until September, is intended to limit the federal government's role in education as appropriators curb spending on education programs, according to Congressional aides. But at the same time, they said, lawmakers want to use the leverage of federal aid to bolster state-

Continued on Page 51

Ala. Equity Case Traps Students in Political Undertow

By Lonnie Harp
Butler, Ala.

Ethel Dazis looks perplexed as a puff of steam rises from a pot of broccoli. As she orchestrates the final touches of the night's supper, she tries to recall how old her daughter was when she testified in court in Montgomery, the state capital.

"Was Andrea going to be a junior or a sophomore?" she asks her husband, Jack, who is sitting at the kitchen table. It is hard to remember.

Andrea is 18 now. She is out of school and no longer lives at home.

Along with several other Alabama schoolchildren, she was called to Montgomery to render a picture of Alabama's schools. Their words, along with the opinions of experts and mountains of statistics, compelled a state judge to find Alabama's system of funding its schools unconstitutional.

The laundry list of problems was "graphic and troubling," Circuit Court Judge Eugene W. Reese wrote in his stern

Continued on Page 22

Mass. Condom Program Upheld	'Just Do It'	Hedging Their Bets	Setting The Standard
Legal experts say the ruling is the first by a state high court to allow a school distribution plan to proceed without requiring parental consent. **3**	A prestigious panel is urging educators to get on with the business of trying out rigorous academic standards and alternative forms of assessment. **6**	Though a new survey shows that states are in their best fiscal shape in 15 years, lawmakers are preaching prudence in spending. **17**	In a rebuff to lawmakers, the Michigan board of education votes to make new state curriculum standards voluntary for local districts. **19**

R

The Tennessee Black Caucus

of

State Legislators

Greetings: Be it hereby known that

Dr. Harry J. Reynolds

in recognition of outstanding leadership, service, support and extraordinary interest in Governmental processes has been appointed

Honorary Member

of the Tennessee Black Caucus of State Legislators

and is hereby entitled to all of the honors and privileges of the office, and to the display of this certificate.

Given under my hand, this

_____ day of _____

ROSCOE DIXON
Chairman, Tennessee Black Caucus of State Legislators

Member of the Tennessee Black Caucus
of State Legislators

R

Certificate of Recognition

Maywood-Melrose Park-Broadview School District 89

This certificate is presented to

Dr. Elizabeth H. Reynolds

FOR PRESENTATION(S) AT OUTSIDE PROFESSIONAL ORGANIZATIONS:

"NATIONAL CHAIRPERSON FOR SUBURBAN SUPERINTENDENTS"; AASA CONFERENCE"; AND "STATE SUPERINTENDENT MEETING"

Dr Elizabeth H. Reynolds	May 16, 2003	Grady Rivers Jr	May 16, 2003
SUPERINTENDENT	Date	BOARD PRESIDENT	Date

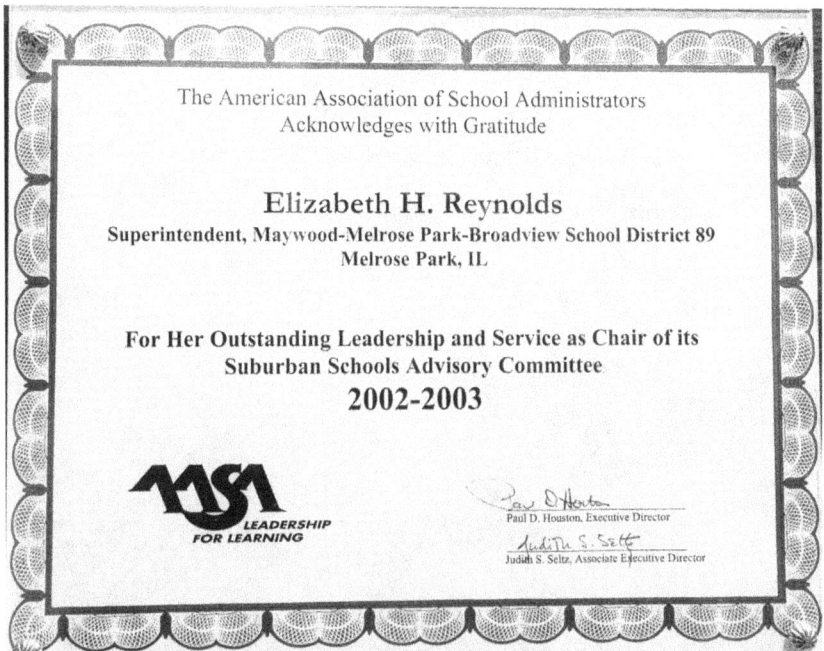

The American Association of School Administrators
Acknowledges with Gratitude

Elizabeth H. Reynolds

**Superintendent, Maywood-Melrose Park-Broadview School District 89
Melrose Park, IL**

**For Her Outstanding Leadership and Service as Chair of its
Suburban Schools Advisory Committee**

2002-2003

AASA
LEADERSHIP
FOR LEARNING

Paul D. Houston, Executive Director

Judith S. Seltz, Associate Executive Director

Resolution No. 604

Governing Board of the Sequoia Union High School District
County of San Mateo, State of California

Resolution of Appreciation and Recognition
to *Harry J. Reynolds*

Whereas, Harry J. Reynolds has served in the field of public education for twenty-three years; and

Whereas, Harry J. Reynolds has demonstrated outstanding leadership during his years of service to public education in California; and

Whereas, Harry J. Reynolds has served as Superintendent of the Sequoia Union High School District for the past six years, during which time he distinguished himself by providing leadership in curriculum development, in leading the district from desegregation towards integration, and in managing the district during a period of declining enrollment and financial restrictions; and

Whereas, Harry J. Reynolds has always held the highest expectations for the staff, teachers, and students of the district and demonstrated a deep commitment to providing a strong educational program for students; and

Whereas, Harry J. Reynolds has demonstrated great skill in involving local industries in the education of Sequoia district students; and

Whereas, Harry J. Reynolds performed his duties with vibrant energy and dedication;

Now, therefore, be it resolved, by the Board of Trustees of the Sequoia Union High School District to commend Harry J. Reynolds for his twenty-three years in public education and his six years of excellent leadership as Superintendent of the Sequoia Union High School District and express appreciation for his service on behalf of the Sequoia Union High School District, students, staff, and community.

Regularly passed and adopted this 18th day of August, 1982, by the following vote:

Ayes: _____

Noes: _____

Absent: _____

Attest: _____
Clerk of said Board

R

CHATTANOOGA PUBLIC SCHOOLS

1872 – 1997

Dr. Harry J. Reynolds

Superintendent of Schools
1988 – 1997

With sincere appreciation for
your leadership and support.

Division of Teaching, Learning,
and Student Services

Presented To

DR. ELIZABETH REYNOLDS
Superintendent
Park Forest School District 163

For Outstanding Leadership
In Meeting The Challenges Of Real
School Reform And For Her Efforts To
Ensure That All Children Are Given
The Opportunity To Learn

Educator Of The Year

J/P ASSOCIATES, INC.
July 13, 2000

R

R

S

SAFETY

Safety

> *"My eyes are ever looking to the Lord for help,*
>
> *for he alone can rescue me."*
>
> *(Psalm 25:15 TLB)*

School safety and security is a major discussion in public schools. This involves prevention and a lot of early planning. This safety plan is a part of your long-range strategic plan. This topic must be discussed with all stakeholders in a school district community. A school district must have safe schools as the first order of business before the academics. If a school is not safe a parent is more than likely not going to send their child to that school, no matter how well the school is performing academically. According to the National School Climate Center, a safe and caring school environment is one in which students feel positively connected to others, respected, that their work is meaningful, and that they are good at what they do. School safety is vital because students, teachers, support staff, administrators, and parents can concentrate on developing and maintaining an exceptional learning environment when everyone feels safe and secure. Every district should have a long-range plan in order to implement a successful district and school wide safety training program. This is a topic that has risen to the top in terms of the discussion of this item about school safety. Since 2014 the safety topic has grown in importance because of the increased numbers of incidents of school violence and shootings. While we struggle to motivate our students at all grade levels; we certainly do not want to worry about safety.

This safety topic is of concern to Superintendents, school boards and administrators because safety concerns distract from the educational environment. It also causes us concern because of the legal implications. A safe school environment is an environment with a culture of high expectations for everyone- students-staff-parents-community members the superintendent and the board of education.

COVID-19

In all of our years in education, we have never been impacted with anything that has been so invasive and disruptive to the whole educational system as the Coronavirus. As leaders we have been accustomed to being able to control most circumstances; however this Covid-19 Pandemic put us all at a disadvantage. This is a novel virus; unlike measles or chicken pox which we knew and understood how to treat. By contrast; this alien illness is new which has resulted in people dying from this fatal illness that seemed to never end. What was even more frightening about this disease was that there seemed to be no cure. This conversation was being heard all over the world. Being a superintendent during this time; the 2020 school year; caused me (Elizabeth) to understand the importance of resilience "during trying times."

For a superintendent; the 2020 school year, Covid-19 and its safety concerns rose to the top of our list. So, what could we do to be coronavirus prepared? The Federal Emergency Management Agency (FEMA) and the U.S. Department of Health and Human Services (HHS) said it could be as easy as following 3 simple principles; Prevent. Prepare. Be Informed.

The district that I served successfully navigated the challenges associated with the Covid-19 Pandemic, my administration persistently worked on two main objectives. One was becoming informed; reviewing crucial information issued by the Center for Disease Control, Illinois Department of Health, Illinois State Board of Education and the Illinois Governor through Executive Orders. The second objective was planning. Once the administration became informed of new changes in laws, rules and guidelines, my administration immediately took action to plan and successfully execute those plans with safety becoming priority. Standard procedures were put in place to assess and respond to potential Covid-19 cases. Our planning increased both by the numbers of participants as well as their efforts. A multitude of teams and committees were initiated such as a 2020 Pandemic Back to School Committee; A Special Safety Team; and A Pandemic Task Force. The School District's Buildings and Grounds Department played a vital role in all facets of maintaining district facilities during the Pandemic in order to have a safe return to school for students if the students returned to in-person instruction or during a postponed opening where our students remained totally remote until the Covid-19 positivity rates decreased in school district community. Our district maintained educational plans for any model needed whether in-person, hybrid or remote. The goal was to provide a caring, safe environment for students, staff and community members.

> **Harry:** Several years ago, I worked for a time for a friend who ran the "regional office," a subset of the state which provided administrative support to local school districts including compliance with safety and health regulations. Execution of these inspections sharpened my eye for aspects of school buildings I had not noticed in the past, except when a physical problem was brought to my attention. During my stay in the regional office, I became very skilled at "spotting" areas of non-compliance, especially those having to do with student safety.
>
> My advice to novice Superintendents, or applicants for a new position, is to do a thorough physical inspection of the buildings in terms of cleanliness and quality of maintenance. Having good information about these areas allows these needs to be included in your early work plan along with instructional needs.
>
> Additionally, health and safety issues should not be allowed to

linger until some emergency occurs.

In addition to physical health and safety, the new Superintendent needs to be mindful of and prepared to address all aspects of the security of the children and staff while under his contract. Safety is always a number one concern in public education. Parents will search out to find a good school for their child and will list safety as a number one concern. Academics always comes second.

S

SAMPLE CHECKLIST THAT WE USE FOR SAFETY CHECKS IN ONE OF OUR DISTRICTS:

Minimum Component Checklist

District: _____ School:_____ Annual Review Date(s): _____

Reviewer Name: _____ Representing

To indicate review conclusion, circle "S" when Satisfactory, "M" when Missing, or "R" when Revision is needed.

I. Concept of Operations.

    A. Description of the school's overall approach to emergency operations.   S M R

    B. Statement about how and when emergency plan will be implemented.   S M R

    C. Identify who will coordinate with first responder agencies and how the coordination will take place.   S M R

    D. Identify who will be responsible for making revision to the Master School Emergency and Crisis   S M R

    Response Plan and for disseminating to all agencies (i.e., principals, first responders, etc.)   S M R

II. Direction and Control.

    A. School Emergency Management Organization (Incident Command System)   S M R

    B. Definition/Assignment of Roles and Responsibilities with designated backup for each role.   S M R

        1. Responsibilities of individuals who discover an emergency or crisis.   S M R

        2. Responsibilities of leader/commander and other members of the emergency team   S M R

3. Responsibilities of monitors who will ensure the proper execution of the planned response.

4. Responsibilities for communicating with first responders, building occupants, families, representatives of the media, and other members of the community. S M R

5. Responsibilities for maintaining emergency-related records. S M R

C. Description of the Responses planned (i.e., what should happen, when, and at whose direction) to address various emergencies or crises that are known to occur in or affect schools, including at least

1. Severe weather S M R

2. Fire S M R

3. Bomb threat or the discovery of suspicious items S M R

4. Structural failure S M R

5. The failure of utilities or loss of utility service S M R

6. Bus accidents S M R

7. The release of hazardous materials, both indoors and outdoors S M R

8. The presence of an intruder, use of a weapon, or taking of a hostage S M R

9. Public health or medical emergencies S M R

10. Earthquake S M R

11. Nuclear power plant accidents (if located within 10 miles of such a plant) S M R

D. Inventory of resources that are available when responding to emergencies including:

1. Emergency contact list, identifying persons, by title and agency, who will be notified in an emergency. S M R

2. Methods for accounting for the whereabouts and status of all children and the process established for releasing students into the care of their parents and others. S M R

3. Response guidance material and the method of providing it to students and staff, including support personnel such as bus drivers, secretaries, custodians, and visitors. S M R

4. Emergency supplies and equipment (such as first aid kits, food, water, emergency lighting, fuel, two-way and battery-operated radios, etc.) maintained for students and staff to use during an emergency or crisis. S M R

III. Training and Preparedness.

A. The description of actions taken (i.e. the training provided and the materials used to ensure that all administrators, staff and students understand the warning signals and know what to do in an emergency, including but not limited to the objectives and types of school safety drills conducted in conformance with Sections 15 and 20 of the Act. S M R

B. Information that exists about the school, such as hazard analyses, area maps, site plans, safety reference plans (See 23 Ill. Adm. Code 180.120), community agreements, etc. S M R

C. Record and results of the required school safety drills and any optional drills conducted. S M R

ISBE/OSFM Guidance For Annual Review Participant Use Prior To or During the Annual Review

S

SOUTH COOK
INTERMEDIATE
SERVICE CENTER

To: Dr. Elizabeth Reynolds, Superintendent, Calumet Public School District 132

From: Velda Lloyd, Health/Life Safety Coordinator, and Robert Berger, Team Leader

Date: November 24, 2020

Re: 2020-2021 Health/Life Safety Visit Report

This report gives a general view of the adequacy and efficiency of school buildings used for instruction, per 23 Ill Admin Code, Health/Life Safety Code for Public Schools in Illinois, Section 180.

Calumet District 132 was inspected on November 19, 2020, as required by Section 2-14.21 of the School Code, by the ISC team of Robert Berger, Jack McCleverty, and Clyde Hayes. The district staff that assisted the team included Steven Corley and several of the administrators, safety coordinators, and custodians. It should be noted that no students and very few staff were present pursuant to COVID protocols.

DISTRICT 132 ADMINISTRATION CENTER and CALUMET MIDDLE SCHOOL

BURR OAK SCHOOL

BURR OAK ACADEMY

~~ We are very pleased to report that no violations were observed at any of the district's buildings.

SUMMARY

Notations about previous violations:
- As in the current year and since FY 16, no violations were cited in the FY 19 report.

- It is apparent that the district is committed to a facilities program of continuous monitoring and improvement.

S

SOUTH COOK ISC – *Region 7*
DR. VANESSA KINDER, *Executive Director* • 253 W. JOE ORR RD. • CHICAGO HEIGHTS, IL 60411 • PH: 708-754-6600 • FX: 708-754-8687 • WWW.S-COOK.ORG

239

WANT TO BE A SUPERINTENDENT?

SOUTH COOK
INTERMEDIATE
SERVICE CENTER

Final Comments:

- The inspection team wishes to thank the district for its cooperation and assistance throughout the inspection process.

- Keep up the great work! Six consecutive years of "perfect" buildings is an excellent accomplishment that speaks well to the district's dedication to safety.

- The school facilities are clean, attractive, and entirely supportive of teaching and learning. The students, staff, and community can take great pride in their educational facilities.

To access the checklist on the ISBE website:
Go to http://www.isbe.net/construction/health_safety/html/handbook.htm. The checklist is found in Chapter Two (on page II-4 of the glossary).

School Buildings must be maintained in full and continual compliance. Please initiate appropriate corrective action. If, after review with your architect or engineer, you wish to appeal a citing or have any questions, please contact Velda Lloyd at vlloyd@s-cook.org or (708) 754-6600. A summary of this report is filed annually in Springfield with the Illinois State Board of Education as required by law.

S

SOUTH COOK
INTERMEDIATE
SERVICE CENTER

To: Dr. Elizabeth Reynolds, Superintendent, Calumet Public School District 132

From: Robert Berger, Team Leader

Date: November 24, 2020

Dear Dr. Reynolds and Staff:

On behalf of the South Cook Intermediate Service Center—Region 7, I wish to thank you and your staff for your assistance and cordial hospitality during our recent Health/Life Safety visit. The pride taken in maintaining your facilities was well-evidenced. Director of Buildings and Grounds Steven Corley and all of the staff are to be commended on their extraordinary daily efforts.

Attached you will find a copy of the FY 21 South Cook Intermediate Service Center's Health/Life Safety Visitation report, which is the follow-up to our exit conference with Mr. Corley.

As you will find, there are no violations noted for any of the District 132 buildings. We hope you will share these findings with your Board of Education, appropriate staff members, and district architect.

The pride in your facilities, the staff care, and the great work you are doing for the students of your community were clearly evident. We hope to provide even more support and assistance in these endeavors. Should you have any suggestions or comments on how we may improve this process, please do not hesitate to contact us.

S

JULY 2020 / ISSUE

ON THE SCENE

CALUMET PUBLIC SCHOOL DISTRICT 132 MONTHLY NEWSLETTER

EXECUTIVE EDITOR: PARENT LIAISON, MS. ELIZABETH WASHINGTON

Dr. Elizabeth H. Reynolds
Superintendent

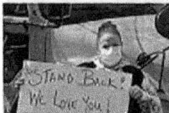

We are prepared to
welcome our students
back to school!

BACK TO SCHOOL 2020-2021!

Dear Calumet SD 132 Community,

Due to the pandemic events, there is a need to keep our families and community informed on a more frequent basis. With that in mind, Calumet Public School District 132 will begin the "On the Scene" newsletter, which will be sent to you more often, including essential and critical information related to our District.

According to Governor JB Pritzker's Executive Order 2020-40, we are in phase 4 of the pandemic and in-person instruction is strongly encouraged. Appropriate social distancing, face coverings, enhanced sanitation measures, and other accommodations will be necessary to ensure the safety of students, staff, and their families. During Phase 4 these guidelines will:

- Require use of appropriate personal protective equipment (PPE), including face coverings;
- Prohibit more than 50 individuals from gathering in one space;
- Require social distancing be observed, as much as possible;
- Require that schools conduct symptom screenings and temperature checks or require that individuals self-certify that they are free of symptoms before entering school buildings;
- Require an increase in school-wide cleaning and disinfection.

Calumet Public School District 132 should also prepare for a return to remote instruction in the event of a resurgence of the virus or a second wave in the fall.

We have sent out a survey to our constituents seeking their recommendation on how we can best serve our students as we approach the 2020-2021 school year. We have also been working diligently with the state. Additionally, each student will return to school having had a unique experience with remote learning.

We have faced many challenges over these past few months and could not have done it without you. We would like to say thanks to our community for your strong support and commitment during this trying time. We are working hard to make certain that you stay informed and up to date with district news and events. **For current information about the district, please visit our website at www.sd132.org.**

"High Expectations Produce Positive Results"

BURR OAK ACADEMY — 1440 W 124th Street
BURR OAK ELEMENTARY — 1440 W 125th Street
CALUMET MIDDLE SCHOOL — 1440 W Vermont Avenue

FALL 2020 / ISSUE 20

BEHIND THE SCENES

CALUMET PUBLIC SCHOOL DISTRICT 132 MONTHLY NEWSLETTER

EXECUTIVE EDITOR: PARENT LIAISON, MS. ELIZABETH WASHINGTON

Superintendent
Dr. Elizabeth H. Reynolds

WE ARE IN THIS TOGETHER!
Superintendent Dr. Elizabeth H. Reynolds

EMBRACE THE JOURNEY!

We're continuing with remote learning...

As we continue to monitor the pandemic closely, the safety of our community is our priority. Our District recently surveyed the families of students that attend School District 132, and an overwhelming 80% of our parents agreed that they felt the need to continue remote learning, as this is an integral part of keeping our students and families safe. As a reminder, I encourage parents to remember that setting aside time to assist your children with their E-Learning process is paramount. Assisting them with their homework, communicating with their teachers, and getting them involved with extracurricular activities will help increase their abilities to do well academically and socially!

We must continue to remain calm, positive, and embrace the journey! Although our world has changed, we are blessed enough to be able to adapt. We must continue to strive and thrive. We must continue to support our students and make academic success a priority. The Calumet Public School District 132 staff is prepared and ready to help sustain our goals for the students.

HIGH EXPECTATIONS PRODUCE POSITIVE RESULTS!

S

S

T

TENACITY

Tenacity

> *"Nevertheless he who stands steadfast in his heart, having no necessity, but has power over his own will, and has so determined in his heart that he will keep his virgin, does well"*
>
> *(1 Corinthians 7:37 NKJV)*

In the scripture above, Paul shows that a person who can control his or her passions and desires has a tenacious spirit. A tenacious person is an individual who holds on firmly to an idea or a thing very strongly. Tenacity is a great quality to own, especially if you are a Superintendent and you are trying something challenging that takes a while to complete. Some synonyms for tenacity are persistence, chutzpah, determination, guts, firmness, perseverance, courage, grit, spunk, obduracy, moxie, steadfast, resolve, backbone, and intestinal fortitude.

In this era of constant change, Angela Duckworth, Professor of Psychology at the University of Pennsylvania, may have figured it out: the most essential ingredient in leadership is grit. She states that grit matters just as much as, if not more than, both talent and luck to achieving extraordinary things. What is grit? Duckworth defines it as "passion and perseverance for long-term goals." Superintendents who perform better are those who stay the course in the face of adversity and are motivated by goals much larger than themselves. They're motivated because the students' lives are at stake.

In one school district that I (Elizabeth) served, I knew there were so many challenges when I accepted the position that I decided the only way to go was up. The district could not have been any more needy, but I looked at every single challenge as an opportunity. My team and I, along with the backing of the Board of Education, decided to dissect the long-range plan with the intention of strategically working to attack the short-term plan. It reminds me of the saying when you have so many challenges at hand: "How do you eat an elephant? You take one bite at a time."

As Ralph Waldo Emerson said, "Whatever you do, you need courage. Whatever course you decide upon, there is always someone to tell you that you are wrong. There are always difficulties arising that tempt you to believe your critics are right. To map out a course of action and follow it to an end requires some of the same courage that a soldier needs."

In their book *Leadership Courage* (2004), David Cottrell and Eric Harvey write: "Perhaps the best way to understand courage is to define its opposite state. Some would say the antithesis of courage is 'cowardliness' ... avoiding or succumbing to pressure, difficulty, and danger. Others would say 'fear' ... being afraid to do the right thing when the going gets tough. Certainly, both of those answers are logical and appropriate. Certainly, both of those answers are logical and appropriate. But there's another description of the opposite of courage—one not as commonly thought of, although equally valid. That description is 'conformity' ... letting things be the way they have always been because of the high price associated with changing them."

T

As superintendent, always be tenacious. You must have courage to do what needs to be done, and there are always things to be accomplished in a public school district. Allow your conscience to tell you to do what is right. Your haters (yes, you will have haters) will always tell people you are wrong, even when you are totally convinced you are right. Some Superintendents will take the easy or less resistant path. There will be those people who will sometimes in school board meetings (usually during the public comments section on the board meeting agenda) unintentionally or purposefully create obstacles that will challenge you. No matter how good you think you are, you must pass the "tenacity" test.

It is a fact that strong, effective leadership is the single most important fact that followers admire. This important trait is what separates the winners from the losers. By winners, we mean the Superintendents who remain in the position continuing to do great work as evidenced by the Board of Education who evaluates you. To become that tenacious superintendent, you must have an undeniable, indisputable, and unwavering commitment to serve that community, and to be the best professional that you can be.

> *"At the end of every day of every year,*
> *two things remain unshakable, our constancy of*
> *purpose and our continuous discontent with the*
> *immediate present."*
> —Robert Goizueta, CEO of Coca-Cola

> *"Leadership is a serving relationship that has the*
> *effect of facilitating human development."*
> —Ted Ward

On the subject of leaders and resilience, Steven Snyder noted: "Resilience has long been touted as an essential capability for bouncing back from leadership setbacks.... Yet despite the overwhelming consensus and supporting evidence that resilience is vital for success ... the truth remains: *resilience is hard*. It requires the courage to confront painful realities, the faith that there will be a solution when one isn't immediately evident, and the tenacity to carry on despite a nagging gut feeling that the situation is hopeless" ("Why is Resilience So Hard?" *Harvard Business Review*, November 6, 2013). Amy Modglin writes: "The true grit of a leader is not how they perform during the good times but rather how they display emotional strength, courage and professionalism during the most trying times" ("Why Resilience is Necessary as a Leader," *Forbes, July 11, 2017*).

In summary, according to Bill McBean ("The 5 Characteristics of Great Leaders," Fast Company, January 24, 2013), the five characteristics of great leaders are:

1. Flexibility—"not everything goes as planned"

2. Communication—allow your "strength and personal character" to show through your communication

3. Courage—"the tenacity to not succumb to pressure, and the patience to keep fighting until you win the day"

4. Humility—"being honest, having integrity, and being tough and fair" to all staff at all levels

5. Responsible—when there is blame, own it, and when there is success, spread out accolades among all employees

T

A LETTER FOCUSING ON TENACITY:

Dear Sir/Ma'am,

I am writing this letter of recommendation with the highest regards for Dr. Elizabeth Reynolds. I am a District 89 parent, as well as the chairman of the Superintendent's Advisory Council. In the history of District 89, according to my experience and public testimonies of many other long time residents, the life that Dr. Reynolds brought to this dying district is breath taking. She introduced a level of High Expectations and Quality Education that people of this community had never envisioned. She is eloquent, efficient, and a woman of truth and principle. Yet, she is personable, friendly and down to earth. Under stress, her elegance, sophistication and professionalism always remained in tact. She radiates confidence in her abilities. The school district that attracts her attention, should consider it a blessing to receive an offer of her services. She is the first Superintendent in the history of this district, who has displayed sincere concern for our children's future, through implemented actions, not idle talk. Through her careful choice and placement of administrators, and mandatory training of teachers, she was able to implement programs (Direct Instruction's Reading/Saxon Math) that have our Kindergarteners reading, and our 8th graders doing pre-algebra for the first time in the history of District 89. As a true Educator, Dr. Reynold's believes in not only meeting state standards, but exceeding state standards. She does not see 50% of students meeting the State standards as being successful. She sees it as 50% of the students being failed by those responsible for educating them. As administrators, teachers, and parents, we are all held accountable for our children's educational future, is the aura she displays. The term gifted child belongs to all children, in Dr. Reynolds's eyes. With quality leadership, appropriate instructional material, and effective teaching, she is confident that all children can exceed their potential limit. Dr. Reynolds has opened her doors to the parents, and invites parental input in all aspects of our children's learning environment. Instructional sessions, and materials are a must for parents. According to Dr. Reynolds, parents are an important component in the formula of educational success for our children. I've never met a Superintendent with the dedication and seriousness this lady has displayed. She has sacrificed her own Saturdays, to come to the district and teach, in order to prepare our children for the ISAT test. She promoted family involvement by opening up a Family Educational Center for after school community activities. She does not believe that learning stops at 3:00 when the bell rings. Opening up the schools during our "Put Your Heart into Education" event, allowed us, as parents to tour the schools, so that we could experience the learning environment of our children, with hopes of drawing more parental interest and involvement in their studies. It saddens us as parents that Dr. Reynolds has to leave us, but we understand and respect the circumstances that led to her decision. Dr. Reynolds has the formula for a completely balanced and successful learning environment. She has proven herself to the parents of this district through the progress of our children. In just one year's time, Dr. Reynolds and the 2002/2003 school board made extraordinary things happen for the greater good of our community and our children. If you are looking for someone who has dedication, loyalty, commitment, sincerity and love for all children, then you are looking for Dr. Elizabeth Reynolds.

With Most Sincerity,

Debbie Muhammad

Superintendent's Advisory Council Chairman

T

Eric Harvey and Steve Ventura, Leadership Lessons (2008)

"Leadership Is Determination"

"Leadership Is Self-Control"

"Leadership Is Loyalty"

"Leadership Is Looking Out for Others."

"Leadership Is Empowerment"

"Leadership Is Action"

"Leadership Is Endurance'

"Leadership Is Example"

"Leadership Is Attitude"

"Leadership Is Authority"

"Leadership Is Dependability"

"Leadership Is Determination"

"Leadership Is Developing Others"

WANT TO BE A SUPERINTENDENT?

T

2254

U

"Humility is not thinking less of yourself, but thinking more of yourself less."

—*C. S. Lewis*

Unity

> *"Till we all come in the unity of the faith,*
> *and of the knowledge of the Son of God,*
> *unto a perfect man, unto the measure of the*
> *stature of the fullness of Christ."*
> *(Ephesians 4:13 KJV)*

Pulling together as a team is important. The team involves the Board of Education and the Superintendent. An effective school board pulls together. The Superintendent's task is to keep all board members informed and to keep their mind fixed on what is best for all students and why we are here.

Because board members are elected officials and many of them have full-time jobs, it is essential that the Superintendent maintains open, constant, and honest communication. This has to be continuous and must be done with all board members, because it can be a problem if this does not occur. Excluded board members will think that you are not taking an equal interest in them. Board of Education members tend to get upset, which can cause a serious problem. As a new Superintendent, upon accepting the position, always have a serious dialogue with the full board first, then with individual board members, with a set agenda in mind. We meet with each board member individually to forge a good working relationship with all board members, not just the president. Usually the dialogue consists of several breakfast or lunch meetings.

The meeting with the full board may include a facilitator who can assist in processing different issues that may arise. From time to time, it is useful to have a full board meeting or retreat to discuss the progress made in the district relative to the master plan (the strategic plan) and any other issues that might surface. These meetings may occur every quarter, and they may be on a Saturday morning (breakfast) or a Friday afternoon (dinner)—weekends are usually most convenient for all board members. The meeting can have a specific agenda, or it can be non-specific, or it can be an open agenda. I also have a "State of the District" meeting every school year to report out to the board and the constituents in the community.

At times, we have had COW ("Committee of the Whole") meetings. Some issues may include:

1. The board knows that the population is growing and there is a need to discuss how we are going to address that growth.

2. Several board members are drifting into areas of management. The Superintendent's domain there is a need to discuss protocol. This may be a micromanagement issue.

3. The district is approaching the time when the current labor contract or Collective Bargaining Agreement (CBA) is expiring. We need time for the board and administration to get together to discuss what change, if any, needs to be made.

It is absolutely essential that the board is unified in knowing and understanding what their role and functions are in relation to the school district. It is also important that the board knows and understands what the role and functions of the Superintendent are—included in this is the authority and limitations of individual board members. A unified board is always easier to work for as a Superintendent.

What governs the board and the Superintendent relationship are the:

1. School board policy and procedures

2. Superintendent's contract, including the goals and agreed-upon objectives

3. Board of Education/Superintendent goals and indicators

4. Board of Education and Superintendent agreed-upon agreements, for example:

   - Superintendent sends out a communicator every Thursday by 3pm.

   - There will be no surprises from the Board or the Superintendent!

   - Only the Board of Education president and Superintendent will respond to the press.

   - "One knows, all know"—if the board asks the Superintendent a question, the question and response are sent to all board members, unless the person says specifically that the question is a private issue.

   - No board member will knowingly embarrass another board member or the Superintendent or staff. This causes a rift for the team of the board and the Superintendent.

   - The Board of Education and Superintendent's relationship should be respectful, honest, and professional.

U

CALUMET PUBLIC SCHOOL DISTRICT 132

BEHIND THE SCENES

FALL 2016

Volume 7

CHILDREN ARE OUR BUSINESS...

Working Together = Success

The 2016 -2017 school year is off to a fantastic start! We are committed to providing safe schools that promote an environment in which teachers can teach and students can learn. The Board wants to ensure the best educational opportunities possible for all students. We would like to thank the members of the Board for the time, commitment and energy they devote to serving on the School Board. It is a difficult job filled with complex issues, however, we feel confident that the Board approaches each decision in a manner that puts the needs of the students first.

The challenges of public education in today's society are many as we prepare our students to become lifelong learners. Often, there is not enough money to provide all the programming needed in our school system. Nevertheless, we press toward the goal of "High Expectations Produce Positive Results" for all. We are proud of the teachers of District 132 and the many employees who support their work in the classroom.

Most of all, we appreciate parents who play active roles each day in the education of their children. A supportive home environment is an important factor in the success of a child's education.

Sincerely,

District 132 and Community Team

U

WWW.SD132.ORG

261

Parent's Orientation

Calumet Public School District 132 hosted an annual Parent School Orientation. The goal of Parent Orientation was to help parents become familiar with programs and operations. Parents had an opportunity to ask questions, make comments and sign up for committees in which they were interested. Parents that attend 7 Parent Engagement Events are invited to attend a very special dinner at the end of the year in their honor for their involvement with the District and their students.

Giving back to the community...

Staff and Board Members of Calumet Public School District 132 teamed up with Kaboom, Nike Adventure Club, and the community of Calumet Park to help build a playground at the Calumet Park Recreation Center. The teambuilding activity was a huge success and such a great opportunity to give back to the community of Calumet Park.

If you want to be extraordinary,
STOP BEING ORDINARY!

David Cottrell, Monday Morning Leadership

SPRING 2020 / ISSUE 17

BEHIND THE SCENES
CALUMET PUBLIC SCHOOL DISTRICT 132 NEWSLETTER

Dr. Elizabeth H. Reynolds
Superintendent

WE'RE IN THIS TOGETHER!

Many families have been negatively impacted during these unprecedented times by the COVID19 pandemic. Supporting students and families through this pandemic is paramount for all of us from the board of education, superintendent, principals, administrators, teachers and support staff.

COVID19 is imposing novel and unforeseen questions for everyone. A common experience for many school districts and families during this crisis is the loss of jobs and income for many families. Our district quickly transitioned to remote learning options to prevent the spread of COVID19. We continue to support our students as we navigate these new challenges.

Thanks to the dedication of our staff we have been able to provide consistent breakfast and lunch through our Grab & Go Program, which provides meals for children 18 and under. The District also initiated the E-Learning Program so that our students continue to learn while school buildings are closed. We are also extremely excited to have launched our "Academic Bus" program, which delivers work packets to our students throughout the District.

We have distributed laptops to students and information about free internet to parents who needed these resources. We are introducing online events and conferences, such as our first annual remote Parent/Teacher Conferences and our Parents' Night Out. Our District will continue to provide our families with their educational essentials during this Pandemic.

Thank you for all that you do to keep our students safe and learning. Lastly, a very special thanks to Calumet Park Mayor Ronald Denson and the Calumet Park Chamber of Commerce for their tremendous support throughout this difficult time.

U

U

V

Visibility

> "But all things become visible when they
> are exposed by the light, for everything
> that becomes visible is light."
> (Ephesians 5:13 NASB)

Visibility is incredibly important in leadership. As a beginning superintendent; you need to remain highly visible; this may not come easy for some superintendents however staying visible will prove beneficial to you in good times and in bad times. When you keep the right people, visibility enables greater certainty when building talent bench strength. Visibility leadership is not just about internal and external people seeing their superintendent; it is about the staff members seeing their superintendent demonstrate the values and beliefs of the school district through your behavior.

Visible leaders are seen, and this makes it easier for you to be heard. Every day you are modeling attitudes and professional behaviors that you want your followers to adopt. If you model through your behavior that students are number one; then your followers will take on the same habits. Visible leaders understand the importance of reciprocal vulnerability; they not only share the good success stories rather they share the mistakes; the worries and the sleepless nights over things that seemed difficult but eventually worked out in the long run. Showing your vulnerability does not make a leader weak; it shows that the leader is human. Visible leaders can enjoy coffee or a meal with their staff; but it is more than sharing coffee and doughnuts. Visible leaders have a deeper understanding of their district, the community, parents; politicians and the students they serve.

Visibility for leaders is defined as:

- Leaders being vulnerable-by taking the risk of truly connecting with people

- Aligning everyone to the purpose and the vision of the organization through real conversations so they can receive clarity

- Being "present" with people when you do engage in conversations with them-so people feel like you want to be there

- Engaging in honest and real ways with people so they feel you are "with" them you are part of the same team

  - Mandy Holloway May 28, 2013, Leadership.

Harry's Reflections:

As a leader, it is important for you to be visible to the community at churches, civic organizations, and parent groups, to make presentations, and to answer questions and share information with taxpayers (most of all). You become an informed, enthusiastic friend and advocate for the children and the district.

A wise Superintendent develops a cadre of informed staff and supporters who are able to make informative presentations about any aspect of the district. This list may be augmented by **V** other informed friends who can fill in when regular speakers are not available.

School leaders should be visible and known by the students at their site. I believe a principal should devote a significant part of his day to supervising, monitoring, visiting classes, and giving feedback to teachers. In order to get to know his students and set forth his expectation of himself, he should have lunch with students as often as possible. This provides an excellent time for students to get to know the administrator as a real person and to learn how the principal feels about the school community.

When I served as vice principal and later principal, I frequently ate lunch with students. On the days when the menu was something the students favored, the students ate the "good stuff," in much the same way my children might do at home. These lunch meetings resulted in a number of effective communications that helped to prevent conflict.

As principal, I often consulted with my elected student leaders when facing a difficult student problem. I had learned that my elected students' officers, augmented by students who demonstrated maturity and leadership in the student body, made an excellent advisory body to the principal. The students could and did advise me when they felt the tension on campus was rising and needed to be addressed school-wide.

Scenario:

The day following the assassination of Martin Luther King Jr. was one such day. On the morning after, I met with some student leaders, who informed me that some students were talking about walking out of school. I questioned them about the purpose and what they hoped to accomplish. I raised the issue that our youngest students (9th grade) were subject to being misled to not return home and instead participate in vandalism resulting in property damage and possible injury.

In our early contact with students, it was proposed that it would be more appropriate if we could plan a memorial that would be student planned and implemented. When the first bell sounded, I signed some passes so the student president could get the planners together and begin working on the planning with the expectation of the program beginning by first lunch.

1. We had parent volunteers answering the phone to assure parents that the campus was calm and they could pick up students if they wanted to or were unsure.

2. Set-up for the program progressed.

3. Some parents picked up their children; others came but remained with their child through the program.

4. The program began at the beginning of lunch.

5. There were some of the most powerful speeches, poems, and songs presented by Asian, Hispanic, Anglo, Filipino, Japanese, and Afro-American students. This was the most powerful and meaningful celebration of an American hero I have witnessed. We did not experience any disruptions, nor were police required to maintain order. Most of the young men and women who participated in the memorial still serve in leadership roles in the San Francisco Bay Area, including Richmond and Oakland.

Because of our belief and practice regarding involving students in dealing with and resolving potential problems in the school community, our school was free of most of the conflict other high schools in the Bay Area were experiencing. All of our students assembled in the quadrangle and participated in this student-created, led and performed memorial assembly. There were a small number of our pupils and teachers who chose not to join the assembly; they gathered in several designated classrooms until the program ended.

V

Notes:

Leadership qualities I have found helpful over my career:

• Being willing and able to help when requested, even when it might not be immediately convenient to perform a task—no complaining!

- Seeing inconvenient requests as opportunities to learn or grow in some important way.

- Being willing to participate in helping others provides an opportunity to expand my network of potential helpers as I progress in my work.

- When required to work with others to complete a task, in order to get the job done on time, it is better to go the extra mile than to waste time waiting hopelessly.

In my early years serving as a regional Superintendent, I frequently was in the audience when subgroups of citizens had demanded a meeting with the new Superintendent of schools to "lay their demands on him." Some of the people in the group appeared to me to be more about showing the Superintendent how powerful they were than sharing concerns and how to resolve them. I observed the Superintendent's behavior—he was attentive, gave positive assent when he agreed with a criticism, was never harsh or discourteous, never put anyone down, and continued listening and smiling and taking questions until no one had any more.

At this point, the Superintendent thanked all for participating, thanked them for their valuable input, then began to summarize all of the input and validate them. He then started to shift his use of pronouns. The people who came to "tell" him wanted to know when he would take action; as the Superintendent responded, I noticed that with the same positive demeanor, he shifted the pronoun to a collective one: "We are going together to help our children. I thank you for helping me to know what you see. I agree—now what are we going to do? Better yet, what am I willing to do?"

V

THE SUPERINTENDENT'S VISION

My vision is that we will create a child-centered school district characterized by the following:

A clear and focused academic mission: A vision of the benefits of a college education and the means of attaining it should begin in District 132, as early as Pre-Kindergarten.

A district that is known by staff committed to high expectations for academics and behavior for all students and for themselves. All students will be expected to be taught at high levels and mentored by highly motivated teachers committed to raising the academic performance of all students.

A district that is known for excellence, whose primary purpose is the development of our children and places children and their needs first.

We must have strong instructional leadership at the building level in each school where principals work to create a positive work environment and are supportive of teachers who are working hard to make a difference!

Sufficient opportunity for learning: The more time we spend on high-level instructional activities, the better prepared our students will be.

Frequent monitoring of student progress: Monitoring students ensures that every child will be given the resources he or she needs to perform at his or her highest level, and monitoring also ensures that no child "falls through the cracks."

V

Extensive parental involvement: In schools where parents are involved, academic achievements levels continue to rise. Thus, involvement provides parents, community members, teachers, and students with an opportunity to participate in the development of educational priorities, assess the needs of the school in the school improvement process, and identify local resources.

A safe and clean environment: The right environment is essential, not only for students to learn and teachers to teach, but to instill a sense of school pride.

A climate of high expectations is a climate in which we believe and demonstrate that all students can attain mastery of the standards, and we believe that we have the knowledge and skills needed to assist all students in meeting the standards.

The creation of standards alone, no matter how good they are, is not enough. To get the desired results, the standards must be successfully implemented by staff that has been trained to do this. Hence, a huge amount of professional development is essential to the school improvement process.

V

As a new year begins . . .

To the Editor:

A new school year presents opportunities for new beginnings, new ideas, new materials, new classrooms, new assignments, new office spaces and, sometimes, new faces.

There is a special kind of joy and satisfaction in planning new activities. Although our grade level or subject area may be the same, the students are new to their teacher, grade level or class, and they appreciate the advanced planning that we do for them.

No matter what our responsibility is, there is always room for improvement and for new ways to do a good job even better.

You may be pleased to know that in Park Forest-Chicago Heights School District 163:

■ Our achievement scores improved again this year (98-99).

■ All staff had additional training Aug. 24-27 in the Direction Instruction Reading Approach. New staff also will get special time and training.

■ All staff will be trained in the Saxon Mathematics Program.

■ We will continue our 11 full day kindergarten classes. They were extremely successfull!

■ We will continue our Spanish instruction in kindergarten this year and expand it to include our Pre-K and our first grade students.

■ We have mapped our curriculum now in all content areas including the Learning Center Curriculum maps.

■ We have rewritten and updated our Academic Content Standards for the 1999-2000 school year and included Social Studies.

■ We have changed the name of Forest Trail Junior High to Forest Trail Middle School.

■ We have opened our new 21st Century Preparatory Center.

■ We were selected by the Illinois State Board of Education as one of 12 standards-led districts.

■ We had over 400 educators attend our summer institute this summer.

■ Our Website is SD163.com. Please look us up on the Internet!

Our Board of Education, administrative staff and union officers are all dedicated, aspiring men and women who have a common goal: to do what is best for all children.

We must, therefore, concentrate on what counts most — *all* students.

Elizabeth H. Reynolds
Superintendent
School District 163
Park Forest-Chicago Heights

V

273

Reynolds promotes positive
school philosophy

Elizabeth Reynolds, superintendent of Park Forest-Chicago Heights School District 163, presented a positive philosophy on how schools should be run during a presentation she gave at the American Association of School Administrators National Conference on Education.

Reynolds shared District 163's on-going success in establishing academic standards.

"All children should have equal opportunity for an outstanding education with adequate funding," Reynolds said.

She said that while social circumstances clearly may have an adverse impact on learning, they are not the major factors that affect children's success or lack of success in school.

"In our efforts to fix blame, we have failed to look at the system of instructional delivery itself — the principals, teachers, superintendents, and school boards.

"What these groups of people believe about a student's ability to learn and are willing to act on are the most powerful determinants of a child's success," Reynolds said.

"As educators and experts, we have tended to rationalize the lack of achievement of children by blaming factors external to the school, when in reality, the real power to reverse poor performance is within our control," she said. "We must be willing to change systematically."

Much of a school's poor performance may be directly attributed to an academically impaired staff, she said. An ongoing staff development program is essential to support a strong instructional program.

"Effective school districts require and foster the norm of continuous improvement," Reynolds said.

Reynolds said that the superintendents and the principal are responsible for driving and sustaining the reform and they must be willing to become advocates for change and excellence, even in the face of opposition.

"The principal's leadership in implementing systemic reform should be grounded in research, including a systematic collection and analysis of data regarding the success of the school or system. The data indicate how and which children are successful, if there is a systematic process for teaching and developing a skill, and the capacity of the staff," Reynolds told the conference attendees.

"School districts should recruit principals who will serve as real instructional leaders. They also should have teachers who are enthusiastic about change and willing to work in any school, including schools in poor communities," Reynolds said.

"Allow or encourage teachers to leave if they do not want to participate in reform. Administrators must be certain that staff members have the necessary skills and knowledge to be effective teachers.

The staff must be able to deliver high quality instruction and be flexible in delivering instruction to diverse populations.

She said the standards are based on the conviction that all students are learners who are active and resourceful members of their community. They provide a framework for teachers and parents to compare what students are learning with what is valued as important knowledge in the educational community.

Instruction must be based on standards, Reynolds said. This kind of instruction is characterized by:

■ a research-based understanding that children participate in acquiring and constructing knowledge and they learn by using and manipulating scientific mathematical ideas that are meaningful and relate to real world situations and to real problems;

■ inquiry-based, reflective, hands-on activities which effectively engage students;

■ cooperative problem solving, and

■ technology that makes learning more powerful, more comprehensive, and more lasting.

Student achievement data are essential elements in the standards setting process, Reynolds said. Data must be collected and analyzed over several years to identify trends in achievement and evaluate the success of programs and instructional methods. This accumulation of data, which is sorted according to school site, grade, classroom, and gender allows educators to assess the effectiveness of programs and change those that do not positively affect student achievement.

Curriculum mapping also plays an important role because it audits the curriculum across grade levels. The mapping eliminates repetition, aligns instruction to standards, fills gaps, and provides a framework for all teachers to provide high quality instruction to all students.

Reynolds also shared research about how mapping eliminates a widespread practice of teachers defining curriculum and choosing not to teach critical aspects of a subject based on personal preference. Mapping ensures that all students receive uniform instruction as they move from grade to grade, school to school, or district to district.

"A sound staff development program focuses on making teachers more effective in helping students achieve high standards," she said.

She said standards-based reform strategies require a coordination of resources, a defined framework to encompass the reform, and district and school policies that support the philosophy of the reform.

Reynolds said there must be ongoing monitoring of the reform effort.

"Assessment and accountability drive every element of the delivery system, including instructional design, classroom techniques, allocation of resources, and administrative matters," she said.

"Efforts and accomplishments could be rewarded, and school officials must have sufficient authority to act quickly, decisively

ly, and constructively to improve schools and then hold them accountable for getting results."

Developed by a committee of teachers, administrators, and community members, the district's standards, which drew from state, national and international standards, provide a set of expectations for teaching and learning, Reynolds said.

They are designed to ensure that the schools meet the needs of all children.

"The standards stress the importance of rigorous courses and high expectations for all students," she said.

"They give us a vision that is based on our best understanding of teaching and learning. The standards guide our educational programs and they help us measure our schools' accomplishments. The standards also establish a level playing field for all children."

Reynolds said her presentation was based on her experiences in implementing standards-based reform in school districts across the country. There are other strategies that are equally as viable, she said; however, standards-based reform strategies are components she has found to be most effective in shaping an excellent educational program.

During her presentation, Reynolds said, "An important precursor to implementing systemic standards-driven reform is to be clear about what we believe about our children's ability to master what we should be teaching and our ability or capacity to deliver challenging high quality instruction.

"Standards-driven systemic reform is an ongoing process. It means a fundamental, comprehensive and coordinated change in how we are doing things. The standards drive the instruction and establish the expectation that all children will be given strong instruction and expected to achieve at high levels."

V

274

IASB
ILLINOIS ASSOCIATION
OF SCHOOL BOARDS

Lighting The Way To
Excellence In School
Governance

April 10, 2013

PLEASE REPLY TO:

❏ 2921 Baker Drive
Springfield, Illinois
62703-5929
217/528-9688
Fax: 217/528-2831

Elizabeth Reynolds, Superintendent

Dear Superintendent Reynolds

I am pleased to inform you that the Share Panel Proposal your district submitted recently has been selected for presentation at the 2013 IASB/IASA/IASBO Annual Conference.

❏ One Imperial Place
1 East 22nd Street
Suite 20
Lombard, Illinois
60148-6120
630/629-3776
Fax: 630/629-3940

> **Title: Exercising Accountability for Results – The School Board's Role**

Congratulations! Over 80 proposals were received.

If the designated contact person has not already been contacted by an IASB staff member, they will be contacted in the near future to coordinate your presentation.

Thank you for the time and effort involved in this commitment. We look forward to a successful Conference in November.

Sincerely,

OFFICERS
Carolyne Brooks
President

Karen Fisher
Vice President

Joseph Alesandrini
Immediate Past President

Dale Hansen
Treasurer

Roger L. Eddy
Executive Director

Consultant, Board Development

NB/jkw

CC: Board President
        IASB Staff

V

V

W

WISDOM

Wisdom

> *Do not forsake wisdom, and she will protect*
> *you; love her, and she will watch over you.*
> *The beginning of wisdom is this: Get wisdom.*
> *Though it cost all you have, get understanding."*
> *(Proverbs 4:6-7 NIV)*

As Proverbs states, it is not wrong for you to seek wisdom, for wisdom is the key to all that is good. Without wisdom, there is no correct instruction and no understanding of what's right and wrong.

Without wisdom, it is impossible to appreciate the value of wisdom or to desire it. Working in a school district as Superintendent, you need a lot of wisdom. Dealing with the many issues in a district that have not been resolved, sometimes for years and years, means that we have great challenges that need to be corrected. Dealing with the many personalities of Board of Education members can be a challenge as well, especially if the board has been micromanaging. However, as superintendent, all of these issues can be rather normal when you take on the position. It comes with the job. The most important that a wise superintendent can do is make sure that all students have an equal opportunity to learn. They are counting on us to do the job.

One of the reasons wisdom is so important is because a wise person can usually control their emotions. Serving as superintendent; believe me, you will have many opportunities to control or not control your emotions. Wisdom is needed and gives direction and furthermore is critical to good leadership. Wisdom lies in the ability to discern how a visionary insight can become a reality. People follow people who have shown wisdom. Research states that; for leadership, wisdom is more important than intelligence. This article cites that people feel strange about wisdom. People always tend to train to be more intelligent but forget about wisdom. To compare the advantages of wisdom and intelligence this proves why wisdom is more important for a good leader.

Superintendents with wisdom can cope with stress and difficulties easier. The wise leader is emotionally stronger so that the problem can be solved in a calm manner. On the other hand, if the superintendent has intelligence alone; the individual may be impatient and aggravated when solving multiple problems and multiple problems may come at you all at the same time. How will you respond? With Wisdom? With Intelligence? Or with Wisdom and Intelligence? The real answer is with both.

Secondly, a leader with wisdom has a positive attitude; is humble and is quick to forgive. Superintendents with wisdom view problems in a more positive fashion. The wise superintendent is not quick to give up because of a set-back. The wise superintendent will not feel negative because a group member is intelligent and has a better idea for completing a project. The wise superintendent encourages staff and encourages dissent; hires people who are thinkers and allows people to do the great job that they have been assigned.

Be reminded of James 1:2-4 NIV consider it pure joy, my brothers and sisters, whenever you face trials of many kinds, because you know that the testing of your faith produces perseverance. Let perseverance finish its work so that you may be mature and complete, not lacking anything.

Harry's Comments:

Serving as Superintendent, do not take the position lightly. The school district may be the largest business operation in the community, so many stakeholders may think the position is a powerful one because many people are employed in the district, and their lives are at stake because they depend on the position in the district for their livelihood. That is why the school board members and Superintendent get in trouble— the district can become so politicized, and many board members are micromanaging and believe they have power that they do not have. Not good! This should never happen in any community.

The majority of the board has the authority to act on behalf of the board when there is a legally posted and called Board of Education meeting. There has to be a quorum at all meetings. There must also be policies that govern the Board of Education and administrative procedures for staff.

Elizabeth's Comments:

I assumed the position as Superintendent in a District in Illinois over 20 years ago, moving from Tennessee, and have now been serving in my third district for over 14 years, which is a long time to remain in the same district as Superintendent, as tenure for a Superintendent is limited. I feel blessed because of the respect from the board, administrative staff, teachers, support staff, parents, and the community. The advantage I had accepting the position in this district was that my reputation preceded me. The district needed a Superintendent that had a track record of success, so that was what the board was looking for. I now have the opportunity to remain, which is a good feeling. I have the support of the mayor and the community. Sending out quarterly newsletters allows us to share our success with the community. Because I pray for wisdom, it seems that the district has been tremendously blessed on all fronts.

Over 20 years ago, I was hired as a new superintendent serving in a district that had been a spotlight district. I was hired because the board wanted a person who could bring the district back to the reputation it once held. Speaking of wisdom, the former superintendent who was terminated had asked the business office to change her contract so that she could benefit from some kind of insurance. Needless to say, that is a real no-no! No superintendent can change their own contract on their own, even if the person is the CEO of the district. This has to be approved by the board; if not, it leads to termination. That is why, as Superintendent, you always need wisdom.

IN 1997.... A DYSFUNCTIONAL SYSTEM

- The Revolving Door
- Phantom Administrators
- Fragmented Curriculum
- Low Student Achievement
- Outdated Materials
- High Staff Turnover
- Poorly Trained Teachers
- Apathetic Staff
- Low Expectations
- Low Attendance

After looking at 10 years (prior to 1997) and talking to the Board of Education, staff and community, it was apparent that the district was dysfunctional. Plagued with unstable leadership because of rapid turnover of leaders. Administrators with titles only or "no curriculum". We had a multitude of problems and excuses. When you encounter a district (a district that is totally dysfunctional) as such , the only solution is systemic reform.

W

SYSTEMIC REFORM IS NOT...

... a PROJECT, NOT A PROGRAM, BUT A PROCESS, which when implemented will deliver the vast majority of America's children - rich and poor - a level of education which will allow them to be competitive globally.

Systemic refers to fundamental, comprehensive, and coordinated change.

Changes in policy, resource allocation, governance, management, content and conduct.

Components of a Standards Based System of Education:

1. *Academic content standards*
2. *Diagnosing the problems*
3. *Addressing Inhibitors*
4. *Capacity of staff*
5. *Staff development*
6. *Resource Coordination*
7. *Accountability/Monitoring*

W

All Efforts Focus on Student Achievement

1. *School Board Policies*
2. *School Climate*
3. *Professional Development*
4. *Instructional Support*

Our Award Winners

- Administrative Leadership Academy

- The Three-Pronged Educational Program

- Put your Heart into Education

These programs won the Golden Achievement Award from The National School Public Relations Association

W

W

X

X-RAY VISION

X-Ray Vision

> *"Where there is no revelation, people cast off restraint, but blessed is the one who heeds wisdom's instruction."*
> *(Proverbs 29:18 NIV)*

X-Ray Vision: Look with discernment at everything.

Another translation of the scripture above reads: "When people do not accept divine guidance, they run wild. But whoever obeys the law is joyful" (NLT). A clear vision allows you to see everything differently. A vision allows you to have a picture in your mind of something that is going to happen. A clear X-ray vision helps you pursue dreams and achieve goals: an idea of the future, a goal, or something that you have in mind that you want to accomplish. A clear X-ray vision will open your mind to endless possibilities of the future.

Great and effective Superintendents must have vision and understand what that means. We have been fortunate as Superintendents to really understand the importance of having a vision of excellence for the districts that we have served. There is also good news, which is that this is a skill that can be learned. It is probably the most powerful tool in a leader's toolbox.

X So, what is a vision? How does it work, and how is it different from a vision statement? Debbie Zmorenski describes this distinction ("Why Leaders Must Have Vision," Reliable Plant, 2020):

A vision statement is a statement of words describing where and what an organization wants to be in the future. It usually remains unchanged for many years. There is nothing wrong with vision statements. They have their place in the organizational structure. However, vision statements do not necessarily translate into action. Without action, an organization has a nicely framed statement on the wall but no forward motion.

In contrast, vision can be defined as a picture in the leader's imagination that motivates people to action when communicated compellingly, passionately and clearly. To be a visionary, a leader need have nothing more than a clear vision of the future. The difficult task is communicating that vision with clarity and passion in order to motivate and inspire people to take action. A visionary leader who clearly and passionately communicates his or her vision can motivate employees to act with passion and purpose, thereby ensuring that everyone is working toward a common goal. The end result is that everyone contributes to the organization's forward momentum.

In order to take the organization to the highest possible level, Superintendents must have X-ray vision. Additionally, they "must engage their people with a compelling and tangible vision" (Zmorenski) for the school district.

We have witnessed more than once how the hectic school district environment of today drags Superintendents into a mindset of "go with the flow." They are tempted to apply short-term focus to keep up with the speed. After a while, they seem to even start to believe that this short-term focus is the only way to stay successful as a Superintendent. They grow impatient with the board, the administrators, and support staff in an attempt to create quick results. They are even willing to lower the bar for themselves and others to be able to reach short-term successes. At that point, they are no longer aware of the fact that this lack of vision might jeopardize their position and the future success of the school district.

"A powerful vision starts from within. Successful leaders take time to listen to their 'inner voice' on a regular basis. They schedule time to take a step back from the daily rush, to reflect about accomplishments ... and about what they would like to change" (Aad Boot, "Leading Change: Why Do Many Leaders Struggle to Create a Vision," Leadership Watch, June 16, 2013). Reflection is absolutely critical. Take the time to listen to staff at all levels. You would be amazed at how the whole school district environment will change for the good when people know that you listen.

The vision of this standards initiative is that all students will graduate from your district with the knowledge, abilities, and skills necessary for success in a changing world. To accomplish this vision, this standards document outlines the content knowledge upon which curriculum, instruction, and assessment will be based.

In addition to the focus on subject-matter content is the goal of preparing students to be life-long learners who are self-directed, collaborative, quality producers, responsible citizens, and critical thinkers. Woven throughout is the fundamental understanding that as students learn content knowledge, they are also learning strategies that prepare them for life-long learning. To support this vision, students will encounter a nurturing classroom climate with high teacher expectations and high content from the beginning of the first day of kindergarten to the final day of high school graduation.

X

CHARACTERISTICS OF LIFE-LONG LEARNERS

Self-Directed Learners:

- *Seek knowledge*
- *Take initiative in recognizing and addressing problems*
- *Prioritize tasks and goals*
- *Work with minimum supervision*
- *Evaluate progress toward personal and/or group goals*

Collaborative Workers:

- *Understand the importance of working cooperatively*
- *Address problems through discussion and interaction*
- *Acknowledge diverse opinions*
- *Assume responsibility for group tasks*

Quality Producers:

- *Create products that reflect high standards*
- *Take pride in producing quality products*
- *Utilize processes and systems in developing quality products*
- *Recognize the potential of technology*
- *Demonstrate ethical practices*

Responsible Citizens:

- *Respect self and others*
- *Respect cultural diversity*
- *Facilitate diverse opinions*
- *Maintain a healthy and productive lifestyle*

X

Critical Thinkers:

- *Select and evaluate resources in the problem-solving process*
- *Use evidence or reason to support or refute a position*
- *Utilize a variety of strategies to solve problems*
- *Identify key issues in complex situations*
- *Analyze information needed for making decisions*
- *Look for "common sense" solutions to complex issues*

Branding is also very important when sharing your vision! "Effective marketing programs that support a strong brand can improve employee retention and morale, help you stabilize or increase enrollment, build community support, and aid the district in accomplishing tangible goals" (Glenn Cook, "Telling Your Story," American School Board Journal, February 2020).

"School districts regularly go through strategic planning, either developing a long-range mission and vision for the district or tweaking one that already exists. But how much attention does your district pay to the branding that does—and should—carry out your work in visible and public ways? Advancing your district's brand is critical as you compete with private and charter schools for community support, students and talented staff. After all, your brand—and how you deploy it—goes a long way in telling your district's story" (Cook).

> **Elizabeth:** There are many different stories being created every single day in our district, and I would not want anyone else creating the stories for me. We have been invited to present our district's story at most of the local, state, and national conventions, which has allowed us to share our brand. Branding is what has given us an opportunity to share our story. Branding is what differentiates our district from our competitors. We have been known as a district of excellence. We take pride in how safe our schools are, how

290

clean they are, and how well our students achieve and behave. From Pre-K to graduation, everything that we do is tied to our Board / Superintendent Goals and indicators. Our slogan is: HIGH EXPECTATIONS PRODUCE POSITIVE RESULTS. That slogan is plastered all over the district and on all communication.

Teamwork:

Each community the district serves has competitive elections. Sometimes individuals will run with a slate of individuals. Some slates will become involved in the political arena with the mayor or village president. When this occurs, the slate of individuals will usually do a photo op with those officials. This does not, however, guarantee that these individuals will automatically win the election.

Once the board election is over, usually a new team has been created: even if only one new person is elected, the team dynamics will still change. Each individual who runs for the board seat has their own vision and mission for their work on the board. No matter what happens, bottom line, the individual still needs to understand that their job involves becoming a part of a team. So that the board is functioning as a team, as Superintendent, I call to congratulate each person immediately after the election, followed up with a welcome letter inviting each person to an orientation with the Board Superintendent and me. Included in that orientation book are the main responsibilities of the Board of Education, the mission and vision, Board/Superintendent Goals, the strategic plan, an organizational chart (the Board of Education has only one employee, and that is the Superintendent), the current board meeting schedule, the Superintendent's communication style and expectations, ground rules of the current Board of Education, etc.

X

'Guaranteed Success For All Students'

MR PF ★ A-3

Reynolds, teachers shape up schools with new programs

At the outset of her third year as superintendent of Park Forest-Chicago Heights School District 163, Elizabeth Reynolds recently cited the successful efforts of the district's staff in striving to raise the academic performance of students in the District's schools.

"Educational research bears out the fact that the most important variable in improving student performance is the classroom teacher," Reynolds said.

"Our teachers' have been untiring in their efforts on behalf of all of our children. And they have been supported by an intelligent and skillful classified staff. Among these are teacher assistants, secretaries, health aides, custodians, cafeteria maintenance workers, bus drivers, and district office staff. All these people do essential tasks which support the classroom teacher, and I thank them for their efforts."

Reynolds went on to say that during her two years as superintendent, staff members have created effective schools that challenge students in ways that are not seen in other schools, public or private.

"The staff is committed to the district's theme, 'Guaranteed Success for All Students.' Furthermore, this commitment is shared by students and parents. It is very clear what we are trying to achieve," Reynolds said.

"People know we have high expectations for all students, high academic standards, and rigorous content."

She also noted that the staff is enthusiastic and shares an excitement for academics and personal growth.

"The teachers are willing to take a chance for the goal of children's achievement and they are looking at cutting edge strategies that will help all children," she said.

"As we approach the year 2000, the district is ready to expand upon the major initiatives that were begun during the last two years. We have laid a foundation for educational excellence. Public education is and must remain a central focus of our commitment. It is the most important investment we can make in our future."

With the opening of the new school year, Reynolds remarked that the staff, administration, and board of education remain committed to safe schools that foster productive learning environments.

They also will continue to implement a system-wide focus on academic standards that seeks to ensure that no child falls between the cracks.

Reynolds went on to say that the district will initiate a character education component this year.

It will be designed to teach children the value of citizenship and proper behavior and it will be incorporated into the successful Superintendent's Word for the Day program.

As in previous years, students will be introduced to a new word each day, be expected to know its meaning, and be able to properly use it in a sentence. Many of the superintendent's words will be related to admirable character traits, such as respect, responsibility, tolerance, and integrity.

Reynolds said, "I am looking forward to another successful year in District 163 and the continuation of high expectations and high standards that guarantee success for all of our students."

X

Sunday, Sept. 12, 1999

292

Tuesday, February 12

CONCURRENT SESSIONS 2:00 P.M. - 3:00 P.M. (CONT.)

PULLMAN
Building a Positive School Culture One Step at a Time
Participants will understand how building a positive school culture starts beyond the front door and continues into the classroom with the students and all staff within a school building. Tips and ideas will be shared as participants think of ways to create a positive culture from day one with the school community, teachers, and students.
PRESENTER: **James Robinette,** LaGrange School District 102
GRADE LEVEL: All Levels

BUCKTOWN
A Place to Call Home
Learn about a New Teachers' Network and Mentoring Program that is designed to recruit, train, and retain new teachers. This successful program has developed teachers into Master Teachers from the candidates we have hired. The goal is to ensure that these highly qualified teachers remain with the district.
PRESENTERS: **Karen Ivey** and **Elizabeth Reynolds,** Calumet School District 132
GRADE LEVEL: All Levels

CONCURRENT SESSIONS 3:15 P.M. - 4:15 P.M.

From L to R: John Perez, State Superintendent Dr. Tony Smith, Karen Ivey, Andrea Brooks-Delaney

293

Hosted a Parent Engagement Appreciation Dinner. Board Members, Superintendent, and Administrative Staff served parents and students that attended at least 7 Parent Engagement events throughout the school. Year.

X

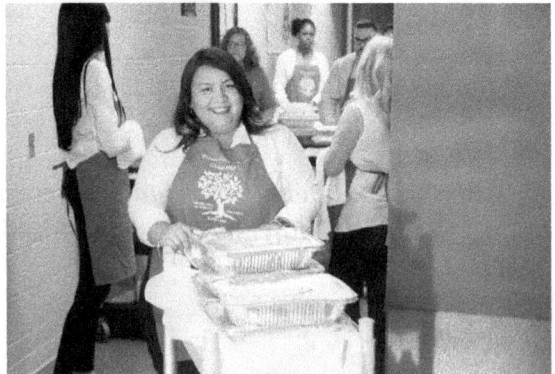

Y

YOU

You

> *"Do not be conformed to this world, but be transformed by the renewal of your mind, that by testing you may discern what is the will of God, what is good and acceptable and perfect."*
>
> *(Romans 12:2 ESV)*

Are YOU reliable in the board's eyes?

Remember that "reliability is the litmus test for trustworthiness."

Are YOU dependable?

"Follow through on all commitments—large or small—in a timely manner. Keep a calendar of commitments, including when you will return calls, schedule appointments, take action on a specific item, meet benchmarks, etc." (Shari Prest, "Superintendent/Board Relationships ARE Public Relations," Minnesota Association of School Administrators Leaders Forum, Winter 2013). Grade yourself each month on your reliability.

Are YOU trustworthy?

Communicate during difficult times to build trust. Some board members can be very demanding; the key to surviving a rough patch and eventually building trust is to work on your listening skills. Never try to get the last word in on a board member.

Y

What do YOU focus on?

Focus on positives to start board meetings, and focus on students. On every board agenda, we always have a standard item that says "Celebrating Achievement"—there is always something to celebrate.

Do YOU think before you speak?

There is always a political agenda that somebody has just waiting in the wings. Don't get sucked in; think before you speak. It may be something that can come back to bite you.

Do YOU plan?

Get your Board of Education as much training as possible. A trained board is a better board. That is why good budgeting is so essential, in order to have extra funds for Board training, which plays a major role in their growth professionally and personally. The board members need to attend great conferences. These conferences allow them to meet other board members, share ideas, compare districts, compare superintendents, and just get away and have fun and enjoy themselves. Whenever I travel with my board, I normally provide an itinerary. I also (because we have a great fund balance) provide them with a travel check. Included in the travel packet is a copy of the travel policy, with details on spending, an envelope for receipts, and other items that make for a great trip (laptops, etc.). In the district where I serve in Illinois, whenever we travel to downtown Chicago, we make connections with vendors in order to make certain they are invited to special events and receptions. Although this can happen in any city, my staff, without a doubt, provides them with a goodie bag filled with snacks and beauty supplies.

It is important that YOU treat your board well. We always provide special gifts on days like Valentine's Day, Mother's Day, Father's Day, Boss's Day, and Christmas Day. Because my third district was the most difficult starting out, I served as Superintendent long enough to see the fruits of my personal labor. Because the district made a 180-degree turnaround, the board presents at every major conference held: local, state, and national. The board seems proudest of the fact that most of them are Master Board Members, which takes a lot of training. Some of them also serve on state committees. This district has a story to tell, and they are proud to tell it! The Chamber of Commerce President, who once stated when I arrived as Superintendent 14 years ago, "I wouldn't have given a plug nickel for that district," is now our best supporter. The students are achieving, the budget is balanced, the staff is well trained, and we are a PLO (Professional Learning Organization) and a Trauma-Informed District.

As superintendent, YOU will get the most accolades when you lead a district to where the board feels most excited about the success. You lead by example. If it is a positive or negative situation, you are the leader. Who owns it? YOU!

Do you have ideas that you think will improve the lives of all children? Would you like to have a positive influence on individuals in a school district/community? Are you willing to be the face of the school district? Are you willing to do what it takes to move a district forward? All of these questions should be answered prior to accepting the position.

So, you have your goal set on becoming a superintendent? Now what? Since this is an extremely audacious goal, and may take some time to achieve; what preparations have you made? You may set up smaller goals along the way or you may already be prepared. If you know that you are not yet prepared; it would be wise to set goals for yourself. There is a goal setting system called SMART (Specific, Measurable, Achievable, Realistic, and Time-based. Specify your goal. For instance, say "I want to become A Superintendent." Stay Smart Along the Way...In the case of wanting to assume this position, you need to acquire strong leadership skills, You need to have the appropriate graduate classes, you need to talk to superintendents/

leaders about their leadership styles and experiences. Do your own research to find information on how to become a superintendent that everyone will want to follow?

It is never too early to start learning not only about what it means to be a superintendent; but more importantly-an effective superintendent. Leadership Network by Greg B.

ADMINISTRATIVE LEADERSHIP ACADEMY

We organized and continued academies over our tenure as Superintendents. See next page for sample agenda:

ADMINISTRATIVE LEADERSHIP ACADEMY

SAMPLE AGENDA

AGENDA

September: Welcome/Overview/Introductions
Purpose
What Makes A Leader?
Preparing Yourself for A Leadership Position
New Focus on Leadership

The Principal Difference
Staying Focused When Everything Is Changing
The Principal's Role In Change

Making Data-Driven Decisions
Why Data Notebooks?
School Leadership Information

TLC – Teaching/Learning/Children
Straight Talk About Teaching and Learning
With Children
Creating Effective Schools

The Role of Results-Oriented Staff Development
Shadowing

How the Budge and Building & Grounds Impact
Student Achievement

Evaluation/Graduation

Y

Calumet Public School
District 132

END OF YEAR
PROGRESS REPORT

April 2009 through June 2009

Dr. Elizabeth H. Reynolds
Superintendent

"High Expectations Produce
Positive Results!"

Superintendent Dr. Elizabeth H. Reynolds
and Board President Karen Ivey

Z

ZEAL

Zeal

> *"Never be lacking in zeal, but keep*
> *your spiritual fervor, serving the Lord."*
> *(Romans 12:11 NIV)*

"Determine what specific goal you want to achieve.
Then dedicate yourself to its attainment with
unswerving singleness of purpose, the trenchant zeal
of a crusader" (Paul J. Meyer).

Live and work with passion and zeal. Serving in a community, village, city, county, or state as Superintendent is as great a position as anyone can have. We always looked forward to beginning each school year with a large open community forum, usually held at one of our largest facilities (high school). The forum is held to open the year with our vision or revisited vision after each successive school year. This sets the tone for the year. The next meeting is the gathering with elected officials such as the mayor or state representative. There will always be opportunities to share your excitement with different groups of individuals in your school district. Use every chance you get. It will always bear good fruit, so to speak, and stimulate a desire for some people to complete their education.

Early in the year 2020, a news report surfaced out of China that a cluster of pneumonia cases in the central city of Wuhan may be due to a new type of coronavirus. The World Health Organization said at the time that it was still assessing the extent of the outbreak

Z

and noted that there were no reports of novel coronavirus outside Wuhan. In so many words; things subsequently went downhill from there. As we know the situation changed drastically. Millions of people became infected and thousands have died. The majority of states in the United States adopted some sort of shelter-in-place order.

For many people; life seemed to be at a standstill, while frontline workers faced a frightening new normal. While the Center For Disease Control and Prevention initially urged people to opt for an elbow bump over a handshake; greetings have now altogether become a no go. Americans have been asked to maintain social distancing, or 6 feet, at all times and the majority of people have been asked not to leave their homes except for essential needs such as medical care, groceries or exercise. Ella Tores April 10,2020

Major cities, including New York, Boston, Miami, Chicago, Houston, San Diego, and San Francisco, closed schools for extended periods, with at least 55.1 million students impacted nationwide, according to Education Week.

Teleschooling has been adopted for many students across the country. And for the working world, many companies have implemented telework policies. Serving as superintendent during this 2020 school year has been a year to remember; a year full of surprises; that not one of us asked for. Along with trying to convince teachers to motivate their students who may be at home learning remotely; across the country we are dealing with Racial tensions; Black Lives matter Protest and an Election that was Traumatizing for many students and Educators across the country.

As superintendent; what do you do when you are trained to control the most difficult situations. Yet over the 2020 school year you are dealing with a virus and all of the mandates expected of you. You are furthermore told to implement policies and directives just hoping and praying that my district will not lose our students. What **Z** teachers and staff experienced is what anxiety does to us; it makes us crazy. I realized that we could either use our stress in a productive way or allow it to spiral out of control. As superintendent; I have continued to try to motivate my leaders and teachers; by being honest with them. I have shared with my cabinet team that I do not have answers; this time we will just have to plow through this together. Since I am a Christian: I have continued to pray for my staff and board and for my students. Have I been afraid? You bet! However, with the grace of GOD and my faith in what I know HE can do: I have not lost my ZEAL. And my district has continued to thrive!

Z

MISSION STATEMENT
SAMPLE

In pursuit of academic excellence, the mission of our District is to form a partnership with family, community, and the educational staff to develop academic, social, physical, emotional, and cultural needs of all students.

The educators of our District will:

Teach a standards-based curriculum and provide diverse learning experiences that meet the academic, social, physical, emotional, and cultural needs of all students.

We resolve to provide students with a supportive environment that is safe, respectful and responsible.

Academically, we will promote the development of literate, motivated and independent thinking, problem solvers.

Socially, we will promote the development of responsible citizens who are honest, kind, tolerant and empathetic.

Physically and Emotionally, we will promote the idea of learning to maintain a healthy and productive lifestyle.

Culturally, we will promote respect of cultural diversity, diverse opinions, others and self.

Z

OUTCOMES FROM
A BOARD/SUPERINTENDENT RETREAT

Immediate:

- Establish clear lines of communication, to establish the ways in which the Board of Education will communicate between and among themselves and the Superintendent, to keep everyone aware of what is happening in the district

- Develop an agenda of work that takes us through the end of the school year

- Come together as one unit with common goals and ideas

- Put the past in the past, realizing that to move our system forward we must take the first steps with ourselves

- Get a better understanding of the direction everyone wants to go for our system

- See how this new team fits together

- Trust each other

- For all board members and the Superintendent to leave with a shared commitment to pursue a system of excellence and improved or heightened credibility with all community stakeholders

Long-term:

- Develop a seamless environment where students are the focus of all decisions and where learning can occur at all levels within this system

- Better understand what needs to be done to improve education of the students in the district

- Build a top-notch team working together to move the system forward in a positive direction

Z

- Raise the achievement level of all students so they can become productive citizens and compete with others anywhere

- Set goals for the students

- For all board members and the Superintendent to have a shared commitment to purse a system of excellence and improved or heightened credibility with all community stakeholders

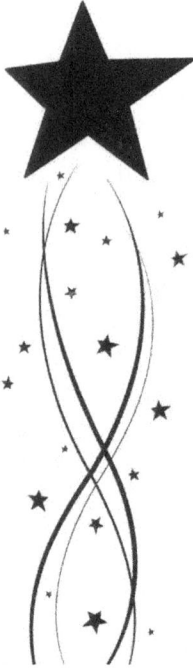

Illinois Chapter/National School Public Relations Association
2020 Distinguished Service Award of Excellence

Presented to
Dr. Elizabeth H. Reynolds
Calumet Public School District 132
AdministratorTeam

For enhancing the understanding and support of public education,
thereby benefiting our schools, students and communities.

Presented this 18th day of June 2020

Kristine Liptrot, APR | INSPRA President

Superintendent's Prayer

Our Father, in the name of Jesus, I thank you for the opportunity to serve the children and the people of our community. Thank you for giving me the intellect and strength to acquire the skills needed to work with and direct teachers and administrators.

Thank you for allowing me over the years to have the opportunity to work with school boards that wanted to improve their school districts. And thank you for the ability to work with boards in a way that proved to be beneficial to all students.

Finally, I thank you for your grace and wisdom given to those you sent to assist me as I strive to improve the district that I serve as a superintendent.

Amen

Z

$\Bigg\{$ **Dr. Harry J. Reynolds** $\Bigg\}$

Dr. Harry J. Reynolds is a native of Jacksonville, Florida. He received his high school degree from Nashville Christian Institute, a boarding school in Nashville, Tennessee. He is a proud product of San Francisco State and the University of California at Berkley. He earned his B.A. in Social Science and his M.A. in Counseling, both at San Francisco State College. He holds a Doctorate of Education in Curriculum and Instruction from the School of Education at the University of California at Berkley and served in the United States Army as a teacher of army medics. He served as a teacher, counselor, dean, district office administrator, high school principal, and superintendent.

Dr. Reynolds served as regional superintendent in Oakland, California, and as superintendent for over twenty years in three states. (California. Tennessee and Illinois). While serving as superintendent, he established nationally recognized schools as he has presented at major conferences all over the country. He has also worked as a consultant for the National Science Foundation. Dr. Reynolds firmly believes that serving as a superintendent is one of the most demanding yet rewarding professional positions that you can hold. Your staying power as superintendent will assent from following the practical steps outlined the A to Z Guide in this book.

Dr. Elizabeth H. Reynolds

Dr. Elizabeth H. Reynolds is a native of Memphis, Tennessee. She received her K–12 education in Memphis city schools. She completed her B.A. from the University of Arkansas in Pine Bluff, majoring in elementary education, and received her master's degree from the University of Kansas with a major in reading. She took postgraduate courses at the University of Knoxville.

Dr. Reynolds holds a Doctorate of Education Degree in Educational Leadership from the College of Education at Vanderbilt University. Additional post-doctorate work was done as a part of the Institute on Active Learning in Middle Schools at Harvard University. Dr. Reynolds completed the National Superintendent's Prepared Program, and the National Staff Development Council.

She has served as a teacher, district office administrators, and assistant superintendent in Tennessee. She has served as a Superintendent for over 20 years in three Illinois school districts. Dr. Reynolds has also worked as an adjunct professor at two universities, University of Tennessee and Chicago State University. As outlined in the book, Dr. Reynolds understands that the average tenure for a superintendent can be reasonably short; therefore this book will provide for you the knowledge and right strategies needed to attain, maintain, and retain the position.

BOOKS AVAILABLE ONLINE

BOOKS AVAILABLE ONLINE

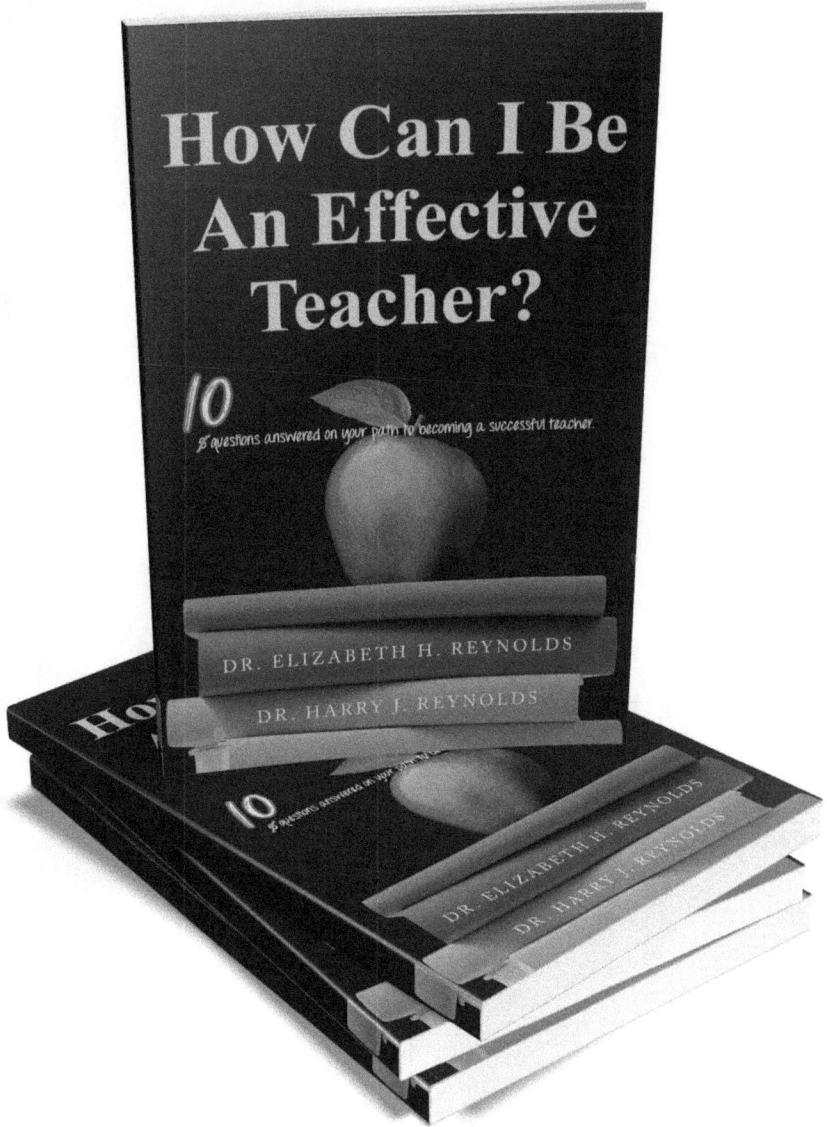

Z

www.ingramcontent.com/pod-product-compliance
Lightning Source LLC
Chambersburg PA
CBHW070554100426
42744CB00006B/268